Mexican Drug Groups in Chicago

Chuck Baumgartner

Copyright © 2018 by Chuck Baumgartner.

All rights reserved. No part of this publication may be reproduced, distributed or transmitted in any form or by any means, including photocopying, recording, or other electronic or mechanical methods, without the prior written permission of the publisher, except in the case of brief quotations embodied in critical reviews and certain other noncommercial uses permitted by copyright law. For permission requests, write to the publisher, addressed "Attention: Permissions Coordinator," at the email address below.

ccbchicago@aol.com

Mexican Drug Groups in Chicago
- Chuck Baumgartner. —1st ed.

Paperback: 978-1-7323700-0-5
eBook: 978-1-7323700-1-2

Contents

Introduction 1
Part One **11**
Chapter 1 12
Chapter 2 18
Chapter 3 24
Chapter 4 26
Chapter 5 30
Chapter 6 38
Chapter 7 44
Chapter 8 51
Part Two **55**
Chapter 1 57
Chapter 2 60
Chapter 3 67
Chapter 4 74
Chapter 5 87
Chapter 6 94
Chapter 7 102
Chapter 8 107
Chapter 9 113
Chapter 10 117
Chapter 11 124
Chapter 12 129
Chapter 13 140
Chapter 14 143
Chapter 15 147
Chapter 16 150
Chapter 17 159
Chapter 18 165
Chapter 19 172
Acknowledgements and Sources 177
About the Author 179

Introduction

The city of Chicago has always been a major hub in the transportation of legitimate cargo. It has also been a major hub for the trafficking of cocaine, heroin, methamphetamine and marijuana. Most, if not all, major Mexican drug cartels have a presence in Chicago.

Although the methods of smuggling cocaine across the U.S./Mexico border and into the interior of the U.S. vary, the structure of drug trafficking groups is similar across all cartels. Every cartel is structured to insulate and protect their various cell groups from penetration by law enforcement. (I will use the terms "cartel," "drug trafficking group" or "organization" interchangeably for aesthetic reasons. They mean the same thing.) This book will describe the investigations of two separate Mexican drug trafficking organizations to illustrate the similarities of their trafficking structures and operations. Both investigations were conducted by the U.S. Drug Enforcement Administration ("DEA") in Chicago.

Every cartel establishes three groups to operate in the U.S., in this case, Chicago. One group, the transportation group, is responsible for smuggling cocaine to Chicago. Cocaine, which is always packaged in kilogram amounts at the wholesale level, is transported in a variety of ways. It can be concealed among a load of legitimate cargo on tractor-trailers or it can be transported in vehicles that contain hidden compartments or "traps" as they are more commonly called. These hidden compartments can be located anywhere there is an empty space in the vehicle, such as the side-doors or rocker panels, the space behind the dashboard or the back seat, or the trunk area. The method of transportation and the manner of concealment is limited only by the imagination of the smuggler.

Once the cocaine arrives in Chicago, it is turned over to a second group of individuals who are responsible for storing it in a safe house - what is referred to as a "stash house" - and then distributing it to the cartel's local customers for further resale. This "distribution" group is usually comprised of no more than a handful of individuals with one person in charge of overseeing local cocaine deliveries. The members of this distribution group are hired by the cartel and paid for their services. The pay can be based on the number of kilograms of cocaine that the group delivers or it can be simply a flat monthly rate. For example, members can be paid $300 for every kilogram delivered to a customer or they may be paid a monthly salary, a few thousand dollars a month, regardless of the number of the kilograms delivered. In addition to receiving payment for their delivery services, the distribution group members are also reimbursed for any expenses incurred in making deliveries. The most common expenses include the rental of stash houses, the purchase and activation of cellular telephones, and the purchase and upkeep of vehicles used to make deliveries.

The leader of the distribution group receives his orders from a single person based in Mexico; however, other members of the cartel leadership may have the authority to issue instructions for cocaine deliveries. Once the head of the distribution group receives an order to deliver cocaine, he ensures that one of the group's couriers makes the delivery to the proper customer. The head of the distribution group has no authority to negotiate any cocaine deals, nor does he set the price that is charged for each kilogram, with any local customer. The amount of cocaine to be delivered and the price to be charged is determined by the cartel leadership. The distribution group simply makes the deliveries. They are analogous to UPS or FedEx, in that they deliver packages and are not concerned with the individual cost that customers must pay for those packages. There are, however, some instances in which the drug group supervisor can conduct his own transactions. Examples of those exceptions will be explained later in the book.

Every cartel has multiple customers who are distinct and independent of each other. Members of these customer groups are traditional drug dealers and they cannot be considered employees of a cartel. They make their money by selling cocaine at a higher price than what they were charged by the cartel. Each cartel customer has his or her own group of customers to whom they sell cocaine. Those customers, in turn, sell the cocaine at a mark-up to their customers and so on down the line until it eventually reaches the end user.

After a customer has received cocaine from the distribution group and has sold it to his customers, a third group, also operating in Chicago, is responsible for collecting the drug money from that same customer at a later date. These payments usually occur days after the cocaine was delivered to the customer. The money collection group is responsible for counting and storing the cash in a different stash house than where the cocaine is stored. The purpose of storing the money and the cocaine in different locations is to lessen the chance that law enforcement can locate and seize both.

As the money group accumulates large amounts of cash from the organization's different customers, they are responsible for packaging that cash for transport to Mexico. Every organization has multiple couriers whose job it is to drive that bulk cash out of Chicago, across the country, and into Mexico. These couriers are typically paid between one and three percent of the money they transport. In another effort to insulate their operations from law enforcement penetration, most drug trafficking organizations use couriers who do not know anything about the people they are picking up money from. The courier is provided a nickname and a contact number of the money group leader or associate who will be giving them the money to transport. While the courier is provided with a contact number, the money group is provided with the courier's nickname. The money group also receives instructions as to the amount of money to give the courier, just as the drug group is provided with the number of kilograms to give a customer. The courier then contacts the money group and the arrangements are made to make the physical transfer of the bulk cash. The primary benefit of operating this way is that, should a courier be stopped by the police on his way back to Mexico with the money, he cannot provide any information about the person from whom he received the money. All the courier will know is the person's nickname and contact number, the location where he received the money, and the cartel associate who hired him. He will know nothing else about the organization's operations.

Like the drug distribution group, the money group is paid by the cartel for their services by either a flat monthly rate or by a small percentage of the money collected. The money group is also reimbursed for the similar expenses that they will incur collecting money from customers, i.e., the rental of stash houses and the purchase of cellular phones and vehicles.

Another commonality between the drug distribution group and the money group is that none of their members know the identity of the organization's customers, and vice versa. This factor provides further protection for the cartel against law enforcement penetration. For example, should one of the customers be arrested, he cannot identify for the police the people who gave him the cocaine. All he will know is a nickname and a phone number. Similarly, should any member of the drug or money group be arrested, they also cannot provide any information about the cocaine customers beyond their nicknames and phone numbers. This insulation among groups with different drug trafficking responsibilities is common among all cartels.

How do members of the drug distribution group and the various local cocaine customers find each other if they don't know each other? It's rather simple. Every local cocaine customer knows someone who is affiliated with cartel leaders and associates in Mexico. In most cases, the customer is related to a cartel associate. That customer requests cocaine from his relative and that relative passes on the request to the cartel leaders, assuming the relative himself is not a cartel leader. If the customer is approved to receive cocaine, he is provided with the nickname and contact number of a member of the drug distribution group who will make the cocaine delivery to him. At the same time, the members of the drug distribution group are told the customer's nickname, phone number, and the quantity of kilograms to be delivered. (These deliveries are never less than at least one kilogram in quantity, which is the standard wholesale unit of cocaine among all cartel groups. A kilogram is 1,000 grams, or approximately 2.2 pounds. The typical user amount of cocaine is less than a gram.) The drug distribution group then contacts the customer and arrangements are made to deliver the cocaine. No money is exchanged at the time of the delivery, a process called "fronting." Again, the price per kilogram that the customer is being charged is irrelevant to the members of the distribution group. They are responsible solely for ensuring the delivery is made safely to the customer.

After the customer makes his payments, the associate who recommended him receives a payment for brokering, or "backing," the drug transaction. The payment is usually around $500 for every kilogram the customer took delivery of. An additional benefit for the "backer," besides the money, is that he faces little risk of arrest. He simply recommends a customer to the cartel and is seldom physically present when the cocaine is delivered to the customer by the drug distribution group. He does, however, face a financial risk. Should a customer he recommended not make full payment for the kilograms he has received, the backer is responsible for making the missing payments to the cartel leaders.

Once a customer has finished making payments for the cocaine that he received, he can request additional cocaine, but that request must be made, once again, to the customer's backer. The customer cannot request more cocaine from the local distribution group because they will not give him any. The local distribution group will not make a cocaine delivery to any customer unless it is approved by their cartel superiors.

While this insulated group set-up makes it difficult for us to identify all members of a drug trafficking organization, one weakness for the cartel is communications. Because instructions must be given from the cartel leaders in Mexico to their U.S.-based drug distributors, money couriers and customers, we try to exploit that weakness by intercepting those communications. The cartels, however, are aware of this so they use multiple forms of communication to thwart our efforts. One common countermeasure is that drug traffickers will use several cellular phones at the same time and change them frequently, sometimes using them for less than 30 days. Traffickers will also switch phones immediately following any police seizure of drugs or money.

This frequent changing of phones causes problems for us. It usually takes us several business days to receive court authorization to conduct a wiretap of a phone and that's assuming a best-case scenario. Once we identify a phone we want to intercept, we need to obtain phone records, pursuant to a subpoena, from the responsible phone company. We then prepare, in conjunction with the U.S. Attorney's Office, an affidavit detailing the probable cause – the same level of proof needed to obtain search warrants - to justify intercepting the phone. At best, this affidavit can be completed in a day and runs about forty pages long. Once the affidavit is complete, it is forwarded to the Department of Justice in Washington D.C. for further review. This review process can take any number of days and is sometimes dependent upon the workload of the reviewer. The reviewer usually requests a few changes or additions to the affidavit before he or she approves it. Once the affidavit is approved, a final copy is brought before the Chief Judge of the U.S. District Court for review. Upon the judge's approval, an order authorizing interception is signed, and that order is forwarded to the phone company responsible for the phone. Most cell phone companies can install a wiretap within hours of receiving the court order.

The order allowing interception lasts for a period of thirty days. Every ten days during the wire interception period, a report is submitted to the Chief Judge summarizing the phone calls intercepted during that ten-day period. These reports are called, not surprisingly, "Ten-Day Reports." The content of these reports includes the total number of calls intercepted during the period, the number of calls that involved criminal activity - in this case, drug-related activity – which are called "Pertinent Calls," and the number of calls that were "Minimized." The term "Minimized" refers to those calls that did not involve the discussion of drug trafficking activity and therefore were not monitored or recorded in their entirety. While the wiretap order allows us to listen to any conversation occurring over the specified phone, if the conversation does not involve criminal activity the monitoring and recording devices must be turned off. The Ten-Day Reports are intended to reassure the Chief Judge that phone calls containing criminal activities are indeed being discussed over the targeted phone and that personal, non-criminal calls are not being unnecessarily monitored or recorded. During both investigations described in this book, most of the calls we intercepted involved drug trafficking or money laundering activity. We rarely intercepted personal calls.

Once the thirty-day period elapses, another affidavit must be prepared to continue interception for another thirty days assuming the phone remains actively in use. An affidavit requesting an additional thirty-day interception period requires the same procedures as the initial affidavit. Throughout both investigations, however, it was a rare occurrence when any trafficker kept the same phone in use for more than thirty days.

Once the wiretap is installed, all phone calls are routed to a wireroom in our downtown Chicago office. These calls are monitored and recorded on a computer. In both cases, almost all of the calls were in Spanish, so contract translators provide translations of the calls to us. A summary of the content of a phone call is typed onto what is called a "line sheet." A line sheet is generated for each individual phone call. A word-for-word transcript of the call can be prepared later if it is necessary for any court proceedings.

Drug traffickers always assume that their phones are tapped so in addition to changing them frequently, they also use coded language and try to minimize what they say in phone conversations. However, coded words or phrases are usually not too difficult to decipher. For example, every cartel uses the words "papers," "receipts," "invoices" or "tickets" as a reference to drug money. The word "girls" is commonly used to mean kilograms of cocaine, although any noun can be used as well. No drug trafficker will use the words "cocaine," "cash" or "kilograms" in any phone conversation, nor will they mention specific locations if it can be avoided.

In addition to obtaining approval to tap cellular phones, we also obtained court orders that allowed us to physically track the location of the phones. The affidavits needed to obtain these orders are less detailed than those needed to obtain wiretap authorization. These affidavits do not require Department of Justice reviews, but they still require the approval of a U.S. District Court Judge or Magistrate. These orders, called "ping orders," allowed us to physically track the location of a cellular phone. The primary benefit of obtaining these orders was that it helped us find the location of stash houses and the residences of drug traffickers, which required fewer physical surveillances on our part. Traffickers are aware of our physical surveillance efforts and it can be difficult to follow them for any extended period of time without being spotted. "Pinging" a phone helped us identify locations without having to conduct an extended surveillance. Throughout both investigations described in this book, our physical surveillances were spotted by traffickers on multiple occasions.

Vehicle tracking devices were another tool we utilized to minimize the risk of exposure of our surveillances. At the time of the second investigation, the U.S. Supreme Court had not issued a ruling on whether tracking devices required a court order. The legal view at the time was that trackers could be installed on a vehicle if the vehicle was parked in a public area. As various appellate courts throughout the country issued conflicting rulings on the use of trackers, the U.S. Attorney's Office in Chicago decided to obtain court orders for trackers in all cases. We used trackers on several occasions throughout the second investigation.

The first investigation involved a drug trafficking group whose leadership was based in the state of Durango in Mexico. Durango is in the northwestern part of Mexico and is one of three states – Sinaloa and Chihuahua are the others – that are part of the "Golden Triangle," an area known for its prolific production of marijuana and opium poppy plants. The investigation was conducted by a group consisting of seven DEA agents, a supervisor and three police officers whose title when assigned to a DEA group is "Task Force Officer" or "TFO." I was part of that group, as were my partners, Special Agents Rich Young and Scott Weinstein.

The Assistant U.S. Attorneys ("AUSA") involved in obtaining wiretap orders and prosecuting the defendants were Morris Pasqual, Chris Niewoehner, Daniel Collins and Lisa Noller.

The second investigation targeted the cartel named La Familia Michoacana, a cartel whose leadership was based in the Mexican state of Michoacan, which is in the southwestern part of Mexico on the Pacific coast.

Throughout the course of this book, I will give my opinion about drug trafficking groups, their methods of operation, and our enforcement activities. Those opinions should not be construed as either endorsed by DEA or considered official DEA policy. Furthermore, there may be parts of the book where readers might wonder why certain actions were taken since no explanation is given. In those instances, I can give no explanation for legal reasons.

For purposes of simplicity, I've used only the nicknames or first names of the drug traffickers we encountered rather than their full, given names. The names of some individuals encountered during the investigations have been changed.

Unless otherwise specified, every city that is mentioned throughout the book was in Illinois.

Part One

Chapter 1

In May of 2003, the DEA office in Colorado Springs, Colorado, obtained court-authorization to intercept phone calls of a cellular telephone used by an individual who worked as a money courier for a drug trafficking group whose leader was based in Durango, Mexico. After receiving the wiretap authorization, the agents began intercepting calls that revealed the courier – who I will refer to as "Lazaro" for simplicity's sake - had been instructed by his superior in Mexico to send an underling to Chicago on May 23 to take delivery of a large amount of drug-related currency. The information concerning that anticipated money delivery was passed to my group by the agents in Colorado Springs.

Based on the information provided to us by the agents in Colorado Springs, my group set up surveillance at a shopping mall in the suburb of Joliet, where the courier from Colorado was expected to receive the cash from an unknown Chicago-based operative. At about 1:15 in the afternoon, we watched the courier park his vehicle in the lot and meet with a Hispanic male, who we would later learn was named Ruben. Ruben parked next to the courier and opened the trunk of his car. Ruben and the courier then removed three heavy-looking duffel bags and one suitcase and placed them into the courier's vehicle. After making the exchange, both men drove their vehicles out of the lot.

The courier was followed to the westbound lanes of Interstate 80. Half of our surveillance team followed him for several miles until they felt confident that he was returning to

Colorado. The agents in Colorado Springs would deal with him once he got back.

The other half of our surveillance team followed Ruben to a house on the north side of Chicago. Once Ruben walked into the house, our surveillance was terminated. Since he had already dropped off the drug money, it was unlikely that he would be involved in any further drug-related activity so there was no reason to continue watching him. Besides, we intended to obtain authorization to tap his phone with the expectation that his calls would help us identify other associates working in Chicago. Ruben was obviously a member of a money group that was operating in Chicago and since he had physically made the delivery of the cash, it was likely that he worked for someone else. Tapping his phones would lead to the identification of his Chicago-based superior, as well as the organization's cocaine customers and potentially the leader or members of the drug distribution group.

While we were conducting these surveillances, the Colorado Springs office intercepted a call over Lazaro's phone from the courier as he was driving back to Colorado. He told Lazaro that they had "done it." The courier then read off a string of numbers and asked what the total was. Lazaro replied, "In pounds, it is 1950." This meant that the courier had just taken delivery of $1,950,000 in cash from Ruben at the mall in Joliet. The courier said that he would be stopping at a hotel for the night before continuing to Colorado.

After that call was intercepted, Lazaro called his superior in Mexico and told him that he had "finished with those people," which meant that the money had been successfully picked up in Chicago. The superior, whose nickname was the "Engineer," asked if the courier had received "two days of work," which was a coded reference meaning two million dollars. Lazaro replied, "It is missing 50 from the two days," which meant $1,950,000, or 50,000 dollars short of two million, had been collected.

On May 24, agents in Colorado Springs confirmed that the courier had returned to Colorado from Chicago. They intercepted additional phone calls which indicated that the courier intended to begin driving the money to Texas the following day.

The next day, Colorado Springs agents watched the courier load items into the back of a horse trailer, which was connected to the back of a pick-up truck. The agents began following the truck and the horse trailer as it drove south toward Texas. When the agents were convinced that the courier was leaving Colorado for Texas, they conducted a traffic stop. The courier consented to a search of the trailer and agents recovered $1,937,667 in cash that was hidden inside, an amount just short of the 1.95 million they had expected to find. It's not an unusual occurrence for drug traffickers to miscount the money they have collected, as they had in this instance.

Despite the loss of that money, Lazaro did not change his cellular phone and he was instructed to travel to Chicago to collect $1.5 million from Ruben less than a week later, an event that we did not learn about until after it had occurred. That money delivery was followed by another of one million dollars from Ruben to Lazaro on June 10.

Although Lazaro had not changed his phone, Ruben did and that would cause a delay in our efforts to wiretap phones in Chicago.

During the two money deliveries in June between Ruben and Lazaro, Colorado Springs agents had intercepted Ruben's superior in Chicago, a man who was referred to as "The Accountant," an appropriate nickname. The Accountant oversaw the money group in Chicago. We did not yet know who was in charge of cocaine distribution, nor did we know any of the customer groups. With the identification of the Accountant's cellular phone and his role in Chicago, we began writing an affidavit to obtain authorization to tap his phone instead of Ruben's.

Following the two money exchanges in June, the Colorado Springs agents learned that the money, after being picked up in Chicago, was driven to a residence in Colorado Springs. The money would be placed into another vehicle which was then driven to the garage of a residence in El Paso, Texas. It was inside that garage that the money was believed to be repackaged for eventual shipment into Mexico.

While we were in the process of writing the affidavit for the Accountant's phone, intercepted calls in Colorado Springs indicated that Lazaro had been instructed to travel to Chicago and make another money pick-up in mid-June. We decided to watch Ruben to see if we could determine where the money was being stored. While we knew where Ruben lived, we did not know if the drug money was being counted and stored at his residence. On June 23 we followed him throughout the day and saw nothing of significance. He took his girlfriend to lunch, bought her ice cream, and walked with her through a park. It was a leisurely day for him. There was no activity indicating that he was preparing for a delivery of a large amount of drug money which was scheduled to occur the next day. The reason, we would later learn, was that Ruben had quit the organization and was no longer working for the money group.

That night, Lazaro arrived in Chicago and checked into a hotel on Cicero Avenue near Midway Airport.

The following morning, June 24, we watched Lazaro walk out of the hotel at about 6:30 in the morning. He got into a rental car and drove to a Starbucks coffee shop at 47th Street and Cicero Avenue in Chicago where he met with a Hispanic male who was driving a gold Lincoln. The male removed several large duffel bags from the trunk and the back seat of his Lincoln and placed them into Lazaro's rental car. Both men then drove their vehicles out of the lot.

We figured Lazaro would be heading back to Colorado so we had just a couple of agents follow him to the westbound lanes of Interstate 80. Once they confirmed he was headed in that direction, they stopped following him. As he was heading out of town, he reported to the Engineer in Mexico that he had taken delivery of 2.5 million dollars.

The bulk of our surveillance team followed the Hispanic male who had just dropped off that money. We followed him to a multi-unit apartment building in the western suburb of Melrose Park. This man was the money group's new replacement for Ruben. The Accountant remained in charge of the group. We were still in the process of obtaining authorization to tap the Accountant's phone.

It's not unusual for a DEA group to be involved in multiple investigations at the same time. While we were conducting these surveillances of the Engineer's people, our group was also monitoring wiretaps in an unrelated, joint investigation with Immigration and Customs Enforcement ("ICE") of a cocaine transportation group. That investigation was focused on the leader of the transportation group and on July 7, we intercepted a call in which the leader discussed the impending arrival of a tractor-trailer load of cocaine. On the night of July 8, ICE agents and our group set up surveillance of a business in the suburb of Niles where we suspected the tractor-trailer would arrive. After the leader and an associate showed up at the business around 11:00 P.M., we watched as a tractor-trailer arrived and backed into one of the facility's docks. We approached the driver and obtained consent to search his trailer. That search resulted in the discovery of 378 kilograms of cocaine concealed within the trailer's cargo. The driver was placed in custody, as were the transportation group's leader and his associate. A fourth man, who was an employee of the business, was also placed under arrest. That employee had been providing access to his company's docks after hours when the business was closed, unbeknownst to his employers. He would later admit to being paid $1,000 to $2,500 by the transportation group leader for every tractor-trailer that was off-loaded at the company's docks. He confessed to providing that access on ten to twelve other occasions prior to his arrest. The transportation group leader would later plead guilty and admit to offloading 6,000 kilograms of cocaine between June of 2002 and July 8, 2003, in the Chicago area.

With the conclusion of that investigation, we now had more time to focus on the Engineer's organization.

On July 10, we received the court authorization to tap the Accountant's cellular telephone. It was through those calls that we expected to intercept the organization's cocaine customers as well as the members and the supervisor of the drug distribution group.

The calls confirmed what we already suspected: The Accountant was in charge of coordinating the collection of drug proceeds in the Chicago area. As an employee of the Engineer's organization, the Accountant was being paid either a percentage of the money he collected or a flat monthly fee, along with the reimbursement of any expenses he incurred.

We learned that the Accountant was overseeing at least three men who were responsible for picking up the cash from various cocaine customers. It was safe to assume that any individual who was intercepted making arrangements to deliver money to the Accountant's group would be a customer of the organization. In addition to the customers we would be trying to identify, we also hoped to intercept the individual who was in charge of the cocaine distribution group. It would not take long.

Chapter 2

On July 17, 2003, the Accountant received a phone call from a man named Ricardo who, we learned, was the man in charge of the cocaine distribution group. As with the Accountant, Ricardo was an employee of the Engineer's organization and was probably being paid a flat monthly salary or a fixed fee for every kilogram delivered to a customer. Ricardo was calling to report a cocaine delivery to a Chicago-based customer. Ricardo said, "I'm behind, but 'Canano' is confirmed." The Accountant asked, "Already?" Ricardo replied, "Yeah, I saw him on 40th Street," which was a coded statement that meant Ricardo, or more likely one of the members of his distribution group, had given 40 kilograms of cocaine to a customer whose nickname was "Canano." Ricardo added that Canano "didn't want that much" cocaine but he was forced to take them by his backer in Mexico, a man we would later learn was called "the Doctor." Snce the Doctor was probably receiving at least $500 for every kilogram that Canano received in Chicago, it was in the Doctor's financial interest that Canano be provided with as many kilograms as possible even though Canano had not wanted as many as he was given. After the Accountant asked for the price per kilogram, Ricardo responded, "I am driving eighteen," which meant that the price was $18,000.

Ricardo was reporting this cocaine delivery so that the Accountant could keep track of the money that Canano would need to turn in. Every drug and money group maintain ledgers detailing the number of kilograms delivered to each customer and the money that is collected. Most, if not all, cocaine deliveries are made to customers on consignment – the activity called "fronting" – with the customer making payments later. The purpose of these drug ledgers, as maintained by the distribution group, is to keep track of the number of kilograms that each customer has received. The money group responsible for collecting the drug payments would also maintain a ledger using the same customer names or nicknames to record the amount of money that has been collected. For example, if a customer receives 10 kilograms of cocaine, that delivery is entered into the drug ledger and the organization knows that that particular customer would be responsible to pay the money collection guys $180,000 in the future, assuming a price of $18,000 per kilogram. As payments are made, entries are made into the money ledger by members of the money group. When the payments have been made in full, the customer is eligible to receive more cocaine on consignment. Recovering these ledgers is very valuable in identifying the size and scope of a drug distribution group, as well as the extent of each customers' individual drug trafficking activities.

Since the 40 kilograms had been fronted to Canano at a price of $18,000 each, Canano would need to turn in $720,000 to the Accountant's people over the next several days. The Accountant's people would be responsible for picking up that money, counting it, and preparing it for transport to Mexico. The Accountant would keep track of those payments as they were made. Ricardo would also maintain a ledger detailing the number of kilograms that his group had delivered to each individual customer. As a customer, Canano cannot be considered an employee of the Engineer's organization. Canano would make his money by selling cocaine to his customers at a higher price than he was paying the Engineer.

The next day, Canano called the Accountant. Canano was calling to complain that the kilograms he had just received from Ricardo's group were not full kilograms. Canano said, "they weigh 988 with two plastics. Take away the thirty-two." The "thirty-two" was apparently the weight of the plastic wrap, so Canano was claiming that the kilograms weighed about 956 grams (988 minus 32), which was 44 grams short of the 1,000 grams of cocaine it was supposed to be. The Accountant asked, "Have you only opened one?" Canano replied, "A complete one." The Accountant asked, "But only one?" Canano answered, "Well, no, I can't open everything up completely because it'll be a disaster here, do you understand?" The Accountant said that he would make some calls and have someone contact Canano.

Since the Accountant was not responsible for cocaine distribution, he was most likely making arrangements for Ricardo or someone else from the cocaine distribution group to call Canano. I don't know why Canano called the Accountant, instead of Ricardo, to complain about the cocaine, but it was a break for us. We now had Canano's phone number identified as well as the probable cause to apply for wiretap authorization.

About 30 minutes later, Canano called the Accountant again and told him, "Look, I got one and I took off the underwear (meaning the kilogram's plastic wrappings) completely. Completely off. It's all nude. And it is short, dude." So, apparently, Canano had removed the plastic wrap from another kilogram and the cocaine weighed less than the 1,000 grams it should have. The Accountant said, "they'll go over there," meaning Ricardo or someone from his distribution group would go to Canano's location to inspect the kilograms.

While we now knew Canano's phone number, as well as Ricardo's, we did not have the capability, in 2003, to "ping" the phones and identify the specific location where Ricardo or Canano and his kilograms were. In addition, both phones were pre-paid cellular telephones, a favorite choice of drug traffickers since no legitimate subscriber name or address needs to be provided when obtaining them. We were, however, writing the affidavits to intercept both Canano's and Ricardo's cell phones but that would take time to accomplish.

As we were preparing the affidavits for those additional wiretaps, we conducted a surveillance of the Accountant and watched him arrive at a Super 8 motel on Route 53 in the southwestern suburb of Bolingbrook on the morning of July 24. The Accountant met with two Mexican males in the motel's parking lot. After meeting with the two men for a few minutes, the Accountant got into his car and left. We did not follow him. The two men then got onto a tour bus with Mexico license plates and drove out of the lot.

We followed the bus to the interchange of Route 53 and Interstate 55. The bus entered the southbound lanes of I-55 and we followed it for a short distance before we decided to pull it over near a truck stop exit in Joliet. Once the bus pulled over, we discovered the two men were the only individuals inside. There were no passengers aboard.

Neither of the two men spoke English, but we were lucky to have a Spanish-speaking agent with us. Both men agreed to move the bus off the interstate to the next exit and they agreed to allow us to search it. We all drove to the next exit and parked in a truck stop parking lot.

While our Spanish-speaking agent interviewed the men, three of us searched the interior and exterior of the bus. We found nothing inside. There were several cargo holds running alongside the exterior of the bus which could be accessed through panel doors. We found nothing inside any of those spots either.

After running the men's criminal history and learning that they had no outstanding arrest warrants, we were about to let them go when we noticed that there was another smaller cargo hold whose access panel was blocked by the open door of the bus. We couldn't open that panel because the open bus door prevented it. So, we asked one of the men to get on the bus and close the door for us. I got on board with him to ensure that he didn't do anything silly like drive off, as unlikely as that may have been.

Once the driver closed the bus door, my fellow agents opened the panel door that had previously been blocked. I was watching them through the glass door and I could tell by the looks on their faces that something good was inside. There were eight separate bundles of cash wrapped in duct tape. The numbers written on the outside of each individual bundle indicated that there was a total of $300,000 inside. When the money was later counted at a bank, it turned out to be a little over $299,000. Another drug dealer miscount.

Both men said that they were unaware of the existence of the money and they both denied that it belonged to them. While these guys were money couriers working for the Engineer's organization, it was unlikely that they knew much about his operations. It's also safe to assume that they did not know who the Accountant was, even though he had probably given them the money to transport at the Super 8 motel that morning. They were merely couriers whose sole responsibility was to transport the money from Chicago to the U.S./Mexico border, if not further. Knowing that they couldn't tell us anything useful, we gave them a receipt for the money and told them they were free to go. One of the men, upon realizing that he wasn't going to be arrested, enthusiastically shook my hand and with a broad smile, said "Gracias."

As I discussed in the opening of this book, most drug trafficking organizations use several different couriers to transport money from Chicago to Mexico. While Lazaro was the primary money courier for the Engineer, these bus drivers were another courier service that he used. There would be others.

About a week later, an anonymous man, who we suspected lived in Mexico, called an Illinois State Trooper and asked if he had been involved in the seizure of money from the tour bus. The trooper, who had not been with us at the time, was aware of the seizure because one of our guys had told him about it. The anonymous source told the trooper that he knew some of the individuals in Mexico who were associated with the bus and the drivers. The man asked the trooper for an e-mail address so that he could send information about the traffickers who were involved with the bus drivers. After the trooper provided his e-mail address, the anonymous man began sending e-mails with the names and photographs of the drug group's leaders in Mexico. In one of the e-mails, the man reported that, when the bus we had stopped arrived back in Mexico, the men responsible for it were concerned that we had concealed a tracking device inside it. We had not installed a tracker, but the men were leery of using the bus again until they felt assured that it was not being tracked by us.

The anonymous man would send additional e-mails whenever he had information he felt would be of help to us. His information would help us determine the Engineer's and Ricardo's identities and, unexpectedly, Canano as well.

Chapter 3

On July 27, 2003, Ricardo called the Accountant to report the additional distribution of kilograms to various customers in Chicago. Ricardo said that he had taken "22" (meaning 22 kilograms), Canano had "25," the Accountant had taken 13 and three other customers had been given a combined total of 121 kilograms. Ricardo said that "39" were left, meaning there were 39 kilograms still available for delivery. Ricardo was reporting these amounts to the Accountant so that the Accountant could keep track of the money that would be owed by each customer. As each of these customers made their payments, the Accountant would be in a position to confirm whether that particular customer had made full payment for the amount of kilograms he had received. Once a customer had made his full payment, he would be eligible to receive more cocaine. In this call, Ricardo reported that he had taken "22" for himself. While Ricardo was receiving a salary for overseeing the delivery of cocaine to the organization's customers, probably none of whom he knew personally, he was also allowed to sell kilograms to his own customers, people who he probably did know. By selling cocaine to his own customers, Ricardo would increase his pay since he could make between five hundred and a thousand dollars in profit for each kilogram he sold. He would, of course, have to pay for each kilogram he received to the Accountant's people, just like all the other Engineer's customers. The profit Ricardo made from those sales would supplement the salary he was being paid by the Engineer. It is not unusual for the head of a drug distribution group to have his own customers outside of the organization, as was the case here. And since the Accountant had been given 13 kilograms himself, he apparently had his own customers and was supplementing his salary much like Ricardo was. And like Ricardo, the Accountant would have to turn in the money for the 13 kilograms he received.

At the end of this call, Ricardo told the Accountant that "another 'family' is coming but it's not for sure." This meant that another load of cocaine ("family") might be arriving in Chicago.

Two days later, Ricardo called the Accountant and confirmed that a load of cocaine would indeed be arriving in Chicago. Ricardo said, "a big fucking job is coming this week" but he did not know "what number" was coming. Ricardo also stated that the load of cocaine would be the last one before August 13, the day that the Accountant planned to leave Chicago for Mexico to attend a wedding.

The very next day, July 30, Ricardo called the Accountant and said, "There is a good number. As I understand, there is 'five to six days' of work," which meant that Ricardo expected 500 to 600 kilograms of cocaine to arrive in Chicago. Ricardo told the Accountant to leave for Mexico and "come back right away."

We still had no locations identified for Ricardo or any member of his drug distribution group.

On the same day that we intercepted Ricardo's call to the Accountant, DEA agents in El Paso observed a vehicle drive out of the garage at the residence which was suspected to be the location where the drug money from Chicago was being repackaged for shipment into Mexico. Agents stopped the vehicle before it could cross into Mexico. Concealed inside a hidden compartment in the vehicle was $692,000 in cash. That money had most likely originated in Chicago.

Chapter 4

On August 1, 2003, we received court authorization to intercept Canano's and Ricardo's cell phones. Ricardo's phone, however, had already been turned off and was no longer in use. Ricardo was in the habit of using multiple phones and changing them every two weeks. Canano's phone was still active but since we had no pinging capability, we had no idea where or who he was. The Accountant stopped using his phone around August 4, so we began writing an affidavit to tap the phone of one of the members of his money group, the same man who had replaced Ruben in June. Since that member was the person who was physically taking delivery of drug money from local customers, it made more sense to tap his phone because he would lead us to those other customers. Besides, the Accountant intended to leave for Mexico around August 13 and he was likely to obtain a new phone once he returned to Chicago.

On August 5, we learned that Lazaro had travelled to Chicago to take delivery of another load of cash, which turned out to be about one million dollars, from the Accountant's group. We set up surveillance of the group's apartment building in Melrose Park. At 1:00 P.M., we watched two men walk out of the building carrying a total of three heavy-looking duffel bags. They loaded the bags into a Lincoln Navigator and then drove to the usual Starbucks at 47th and Cicero in Chicago, where Lazaro was already waiting. The three duffel bags were then transferred into Lazaro's rental car. Once the exchange was complete, the men went their separate ways. We followed Lazaro to the southbound lanes of Interstate 55 at which point we stopped following him. The agents in Colorado Springs would keep an eye on him once he returned to Colorado.

On August 22, we obtained court authorization to tap the cell phone used by one of the members of the Accountant's money group. The man's name was "Alonso" and he lived at the apartment building in Melrose Park. The two men who lived with him, and who also worked for the Accountant, were known as "Toucan" and "Gerardo."

On August 27, Alonso received a call from the Accountant who had returned from Mexico. In somewhat coded language, the Accountant said that two different money couriers would be arriving in Chicago over the next few days. The Accountant said, "Between both they have to take '770,'" which meant the couriers would be transporting a total of $770,000 in drug money between the two of them, money that would be provided by Alonso and his associates.

The next day, the Accountant provided Alonso with a phone number to contact one of the money couriers. The number was for a hotel in Morris, a city about 60 miles southwest of Chicago. The Accountant also provided Alonso with the courier's room number. Alonso was instructed to provide this courier with $250,000 in cash to transport.

A couple of agents went to the hotel and observed a red minivan with Mexico license plates parked in the hotel lot. A hotel clerk confirmed that a man had just arrived from Mexico and was staying in the same room that the Accountant had provided to Alonso.

We intercepted Alonso making several calls to the hotel on the night of August 28, but he did not get through to the courier.

The next morning, we set up surveillance at the hotel. At about 11:30 A.M., the courier came out of the hotel and got into the minivan with the Mexico plates. The courier drove out of the lot and we followed him to a truck stop in Bolingbrook.

At 12:30 P.M., Alonso received a call from the money group member named Gerardo. Gerardo said that he had spoken to the courier and the courier had left the hotel because a clerk "told him that someone went there looking for him, so he left to go somewhere else." It appeared that a hotel employee had tipped off the courier about our interest in him. Unbeknownst to us, the courier had spotted our surveillance cars almost immediately after he had left the hotel.

In the meantime, the courier had left the Bolingbrook truck stop and was driving to various locations throughout Chicago, all the while with us in tow. At about 2:00 P.M., Gerardo called Alonso and told him that "they couldn't do it anymore," which meant that the money could not be delivered to the courier. Gerardo said the courier had called and said he had "bumps on his back," a coded phrase which meant the courier had spotted our surveillance team. Gerardo said the courier did not want to risk "losing it all" so he wanted to "borrow enough so he can get back." Since the courier had spotted our surveillance he did not want to take delivery of the drug money because he feared "losing it all" to us, which he would have since we had every intention of seizing it from him some time after he received it. What the courier was asking for, however, was enough money to drive back to Mexico ("borrow enough so he can get back").

Alonso then called the Accountant to fill him in. Alonso said the courier "can't take anything because he has a 'tail.'" Alonso said the courier wanted some money to get back to Mexico but, Alonso said, "it would be hard since he has a 'scraped back' since the hotel. It will be hard to get near him." What Alonso was saying was that neither he nor Gerardo wanted to meet with the courier to give him money because they did not want to attract law enforcement attention to themselves.

About an hour later, the Accountant called Alonso and told him not to answer any more of the courier's phone calls. The Accountant said that another individual would take delivery of the cash. The group was obviously making arrangements with another courier to get that money out of Chicago. And since we weren't listening to the Accountant's new phone, we were not going to learn about those arrangements.

Following that miss, Canano began to take center stage.

Chapter 5

On September 2, Canano placed a call to an individual named Marco, who was one of Canano's cocaine customers. Marco told Canano that he wanted "eight tickets tomorrow, for sure," which meant that Marco wanted eight kilograms of cocaine. While "tickets" usually is a reference to cash, it is sometimes also used as a code for kilograms of cocaine. Canano told Marco to get "at least ten just to fill up the boxes." Canano said that he would put in the order for "ten" and told Marco to call if he wanted more.

A few minutes later, Canano called a phone number in Mexico and spoke to his backer, the individual whose nickname was the "Doctor." Since the Doctor was Canano's backer, Canano needed to place his cocaine orders through him. Canano told the Doctor that he "might need ten for the dance," an easily deciphered code meaning ten kilograms of cocaine. Canano also asked to "reserve 25 girls" (another easily deciphered code), but he wanted "ten for sure." Canano said he would call the Doctor the following day when he needed the "ten for the dance."

As with every backer in a drug trafficking organization, the Doctor was probably receiving around $500 for every kilogram of cocaine that Canano took delivery of in Chicago. Since the Doctor was in Mexico, he had little risk of being arrested as he would not be present when the cocaine would be delivered to Canano by Ricardo's drug group in Chicago. The Doctor would be financially responsible, however, should Canano not make full payment for the kilograms he would be fronted. Canano, in turn, was making five hundred to one thousand dollars for each kilogram he was selling to Marco.

The next day, September 3, at around 10 o'clock in the morning, Canano called the Doctor in Mexico and said that he could "work 10th Street right now." Canano said that the "guy," meaning Marco, was going to deliver "the receipts for the rent," which meant that Marco would deliver the money for the kilograms prior to receiving them. While Canano was getting the cocaine fronted to him by Ricardo's drug group, he was not, in turn, fronting the cocaine to his customers. In fact, Canano wasn't even expecting cash at the time of delivery to Marco. He was expecting the cash to be fronted to him long before he physically took delivery of the cocaine from Ricardo's people.

About an hour after placing his order with the Doctor in Mexico, Canano received a phone call from an unidentified male using a cellular phone with a suburban Chicago area code. It is safe to speculate on the likely sequence of events that led up to this call. After Canano placed his order with his backer, the Doctor in Mexico, the Doctor would have passed that order on to the Engineer. The Engineer would then give the approval to Ricardo and his distribution group in Chicago to make the delivery to Canano. The unidentified male intercepted in this call would, in fact, turn out to be a member of the drug distribution group working for Ricardo in Chicago and he was calling to make the arrangements for the delivery. Canano asked the man, "How is the house on 10th Street?" The male replied that it was good. Canano said that he was going to put his "brother" on the phone. After Canano's "brother" came on the line, the male asked when he could come by. Canano's brother, who was later identified as "Ahmed," replied, "Right now." Ahmed and the male agreed to meet at a White Hen Pantry convenience store on "59th Road," which was a coded reference to Route 59 in Naperville, a suburb about thirty miles west of Chicago.

At around noon, Ahmed, who was now using Canano's phone in a fortunate break for us, received a call from Marco. Ahmed and Marco agreed to meet at a fast-food restaurant at "Harlem and Lake," two streets that intersect in the village of Oak Park just west of Chicago. It would be our first opportunity to see Canano's associates. At around 12:15 P.M., one of our agents saw Marco and Ahmed walk out of the restaurant together. They both walked to a Cadillac Escalade that was parked in the lot. The license plate on the Escalade was registered in Marco's name at an address in South Holland, a suburb south of Chicago. Ahmed opened the front passenger door of the Escalade and retrieved a duffel bag. Ahmed then walked to a red Mitsubishi and placed the bag inside. That bag likely contained the cash that Marco needed to provide before receiving his 10 kilograms of cocaine from Canano. The license plate on the Mitsubishi was registered in Ahmed's name at an address in Round Lake Beach, a town about sixty miles north of Chicago. Both men then drove their respective vehicles out of the lot and went in separate directions.

We now had one of Canano's associates (Ahmed) identified as well as one of his customers (Marco). But we still did not know who or where Canano was. The cellular location technology available at the time was providing us only with a general area where Canano's phone was being utilized and it was not specific enough to locate him.

Around the same time that Ahmed was taking delivery of Marco's cash, he received a call from the unidentified male with the drug distribution group. The male asked Ahmed where he was. Ahmed said he was on his way because he "just picked up some receipts."

At 1:00 P.M., a team of agents were watching the White Hen Pantry on Route 59, where we expected Ahmed to take delivery of the ten kilograms from a member of the drug distribution group. We only had about a half-dozen agents and officers available for surveillance and we had two objectives which would require us to split our already small team in half. Our first objective was to follow whoever showed up with the ten kilograms with the expectation that he would lead us to the stash house used by the drug distribution group. The second objective was to follow Ahmed and hope to see him deliver the ten kilograms to Marco. We then intended to stop Marco and seize the cocaine from him.

At around 1:15 P.M., Ahmed arrived and parked his Mitsubishi in the lot of the White Hen Pantry. Twenty minutes later, a white Chrysler mini-van, with two Hispanic men inside, drove into the lot. The driver of the van got out and opened a side door of the mini-van. The man removed a white box, large enough to hold ten kilograms of cocaine, and carried it to Ahmed's Mitsubishi. The man placed the box into the opened trunk of the Mitsubishi and then walked up to the driver's side of the car where Ahmed was sitting. After talking to Ahmed for several seconds, the man returned to the van and both vehicles drove out of the lot. We now split our surveillance team to follow both vehicles.

We successfully followed the two men in the white Chrysler mini-van to a house on Columbia Street in Aurora, a western suburb of Chicago. The van pulled into a garage at the residence. While we knew this residence was associated with members of the distribution group, we could not be sure if it was the cocaine stash house. But now, for the first time, we had a place to watch.

The other half of our team followed Ahmed to the west side of Chicago. At about 2:05 P.M., Canano called Ahmed and asked if he was on his way to see Marco. Ahmed said there were "little kids following" him. Ahmed had evidently spotted our surveillance guys. Canano asked if Ahmed was sure. Ahmed replied, "Yes, 100%."

As Ahmed drove through the neighborhood, surveillance agents lost sight of him for a period. When they eventually found his Mitsubishi on a side street, they noticed it was parked near Marco's Escalade. Both vehicles then drove out of the area, with the agents focused on stopping Marco's vehicle since we assumed that the ten kilograms were now in his car, although no one had been able to observe an exchange.

After following Marco for a short distance, a couple of agents conducted a traffic stop. Marco and another man were in the vehicle. The agents searched his Escalade and found 240 grams of cocaine, a .40 caliber handgun, and about $23,000 in cash. The white box that they had expected to find was not in the vehicle.

Marco and his companion were taken into custody.

Since the box with the ten kilograms was not in Marco's vehicle, another agent decided to stop Ahmed and search his car. Ahmed consented to a search and the white box that we had seen being placed into the trunk was no longer inside. Since there was no contraband found in Ahmed's car, we released him. But during the traffic stop, Ahmed told us he worked at a furniture store on Grand Avenue in Chicago, a detail that would prove to be important later.

While it was disappointing that we were unable to determine where the white box with the ten kilograms had gone, we had identified a potential cocaine stash house in Aurora that was associated with the distribution group. We also learned that the customer Marco, whose identity we had just learned that day, was already under investigation by another DEA group and the Internal Revenue Service.

We would later learn, at a trial, that the box with the ten kilograms had been carried into an apartment building on the same block where surveillance agents had seen Ahmed's and Marco's parked vehicles. But none of the agents on surveillance that day had seen where the box had gone prior to Ahmed and Marco driving away.

The next day, September 4, at about 2:15 P.M., Canano spoke to the Accountant and told him that there "was a problem yesterday." Canano said he wanted to know "where the tail is coming from." Canano added, "It could have been worse, but it wasn't that bad." Canano told the Accountant to come by so they could talk.

At 7:45 P.M., Canano talked to the Doctor in Mexico. Canano said, "We had a problem yesterday." Canano said he had met with the Accountant and explained the situation. Canano said, "There's a guy I can't find right now," which was a reference to Marco who was still in custody. Canano continued, "I'm going to respond with the receipts of what I'm supposed to be responsible for yesterday." The Doctor asked, "Okay, of the ten?" Canano said, "Uh huh. The 'work' is already done." What Canano meant was that he would be delivering Marco's cash ("receipts") for the ten kilograms to the Accountant. The "work" being "done" meant that the ten kilograms had been successfully delivered since we had missed it. Canano continued, "The only thing is that my brother (Ahmed) got into some problems. It looks like they let some dogs loose from the yard and they bit my brother. You understand? But everything turned out all right." Canano was telling the Doctor in coded language that his brother had been stopped by the police ("let some dogs loose from the yard and they bit my brother"). The Doctor asked, "But we didn't lose anything? Or break anything?" Canano replied, "Right now, the only thing that got damaged was the 'receipts' on his side," which was a reference to the $23,000 in cash that was seized during the stop of Marco.

On the same day that Canano was explaining his troubles to the Accountant and the Doctor, we intercepted a call over Alonso's phone. At about 3:15 in the afternoon, Alonso received a call from the man nicknamed "Toucan," who was the third member of the Accountant's money group. Toucan asked for Alonso's help in carrying "two large bags." Alonso wanted to know what "the number" was. Toucan initially replied, "One million," then added "one melon," probably realizing that he should not have stated the actual amount of money over the phone. Alonso said that he would come down and help Toucan with the bags. In a subsequent call about ten minutes later, Alonso told an unidentified male that they had "a big one," meaning the million dollars that Toucan had just collected and would be working all night. That money would be counted and packaged by Alonso and Toucan and two days later, on September 6, half a million of it would be delivered to the Colorado courier, Lazaro, in the parking lot of the Starbucks on Cicero Avenue in Chicago.

On September 5, a couple of agents were watching the potential cocaine stash house on Colombia in Aurora when they observed several men carrying dozens of boxes and other items out of the house and loading them into two different vehicles that were parked in the driveway. Once the vehicles were loaded, they traveled in tandem to a house several blocks away on Harrison Street. The men then unloaded the vehicles and carried the boxes into this new location. It appeared as if the drug group was changing stash houses in response to Ahmed and Marco's troubles two days earlier which, we would soon learn, was exactly what they were doing. We now had two houses associated with the drug group to watch.

On September 11, a local law enforcement agency was conducting surveillance in an unrelated investigation. During their surveillance, they saw an exchange of a backpack between two men. The officers followed the man who had taken possession of the backpack. That man, unbeknownst to us, was a fourth member of the Accountant's money crew. The officers followed the man to the apartment building in Melrose Park occupied by Alonso, Gerardo, and Toucan. Once the man parked his car, the officers approached him and obtained consent to search the backpack.. The bag contained approximately $80,000 in cash. In addition to consenting to the search of his backpack, the man identified the specific apartment where he resided, and he consented to a search of that as well. The officers found nothing of significance during their search of the apartment, but while they were inside, our wiretap target, Alonso, showed up. Neither Alonso nor the other man were arrested but the seizure of the money and the apartment search would have repercussions for our investigation. We would not learn of the seizure until the following day and we would not learn the details surrounding the event for several more days because our attention needed to be shifted, once again, to Canano.

Chapter 6

On September 12, Canano placed a call to another one of his cocaine customers whose name was "Darrell." In coded language, Darrell told Canano that he might order 40 kilograms of cocaine for the following day.

Immediately after that call, Canano called the Engineer in Mexico. Canano, who had previously placed cocaine orders with his backer the Doctor, was now placing his orders directly with the man in charge. Canano had cut out the middleman. Canano said he wanted to "finish the project on 40th Street" and would call the Engineer the next day to confirm.

The next day, Canano called the Engineer and told him he was "taking a little longer" because he might "need more 'workers,'" 'workers' being the code word for kilograms. The Engineer said, "You tell me." Canano asked, "How many 'guys' do you have there?" The Engineer replied, "500," which meant 500 kilograms were available in Chicago and were most likely stored in one or both houses we had identified in Aurora. Canano said he would call once he confirmed an order.

Over the next two days, we intercepted several calls between Darrell and Canano in which they discussed the potential order from Darrell. Despite the coded language they used, it appeared that Darrell was having difficulty gathering the money required to purchase 40 kilograms. As with Marco, Canano would not front the cocaine to Darrell and he expected the money in advance for each kilo that Darrell intended to buy.

On September 15, at around noon, Ahmed, using Canano's phone, called Darrell and asked if he "set up the workers."

Darrell answered, "Yeah, eighteen," which meant that Darrell had the money for 18 kilograms of cocaine.

At 1:46 P.M., Canano called the Engineer in Mexico and told him that "the guy," meaning Darrell, had "confirmed 18th Street." Canano said he was going "to pick up the papers," which meant that he would get the money from Darrell before providing him with the cocaine. Canano said he would call the Engineer later to "finish 18th Street today."

At about 2:22 P.M., the Accountant called Canano to confirm that Canano had placed an order for cocaine. Canano said "the guy is supposed to be working '18th Street' today." Canano said that he was waiting while they "check the papers." Why the Accountant, who oversaw the money group, made this call cannot be explained. Perhaps Ricardo, the man in charge of the cocaine group, was not available and the Accountant was performing Ricardo's role. Or, it is possible that the Accountant was confirming the number of kilograms that Canano would be receiving to determine the amount of cash that Canano would need to deliver over the next several days. Either explanation is plausible.

At about 3:00 P.M., Ahmed called Canano and said that he needed "three more guys." Canano said that he would ask. Two minutes later, Canano received a call from one of the members of Ricardo's distribution group. Canano asked the man if he could get "three more guys on 18th Street," which meant that Canano now wanted 21 kilograms. The man said, "No problem." While this man ordinarily would not have had the authority to agree to deliver three more kilograms, Canano had already received the approval from the Engineer to take delivery of up to forty kilograms. Had Canano requested any more than forty, the man would have had to obtain the approval of the Engineer.

Canano then called Ahmed and told him he got "the okay for three more guys." Canano told Ahmed to "make sure" he received the "paperwork for the rest of the guys," which meant that he wanted Ahmed to ensure that Darrell had all the money required for the purchase of 21 kilograms.

As these calls were occurring, we were setting up surveillance of the two houses in Aurora. Since we weren't sure if either or both houses were being used as stash houses, we had to watch them both.

At 4:20 P.M., a Hispanic male walked out of the house on Colombia, got into a white Dodge Intrepid, and drove away. He arrived, a few minutes later, at the house on Harrison. A short time later, another Hispanic man came out of the Colombia house and got into the same white mini-van that we had seen a few weeks earlier during the ten-kilogram delivery to Ahmed. That man was also followed to the house on Harrison.

At 5:00 P.M., one of the men walked out of the Harrison house carrying a box, which appeared to be heavily weighted, and placed it into the white mini-van. We correctly assumed that the box contained the 21 kilograms that Canano had ordered. The other man also came out of the house and got into the Intrepid. Both vehicles then drove away from the house, with the Intrepid following the van.

At 5:10 P.M., Aurora Police officers conducted a traffic stop of the mini-van. The driver, now identified as "Luis," consented to a search of the van. Officers found the box inside the van and discovered that it contained 21 kilograms of cocaine. Luis was then arrested.

After the van had been pulled over, the Intrepid continued a short distance before the driver pulled into a parking lot. The driver got out of the car and began to walk away. We took him into custody before he got too far. His name was "Aaron" and he was the brother of Luis.

As these arrests were occurring, Ahmed placed a call to Canano and said, "They got him." Canano asked, "They got who?" Ahmed replied, "The guy." Canano asked, "Where you at?" Ahmed answered, "I'm heading back right now."

While none of us had seen Ahmed at the time, he was obviously in the vicinity and had witnessed the traffic stop. He was there to take delivery of the cocaine and bring it to Canano's customer, Darrell. Since we had no intention of arresting him at that point, we didn't bother looking for him. We knew who he was and where to find him when the time came to arrest him. We still did not know, at this point, who Canano was since he had never shown up at any of the cocaine or money exchanges we had intercepted over his phone. Ahmed handled that. We considered following Ahmed since he could have led us to Canano, but we felt it wasn't worth the risk. It was extremely likely that Ahmed would have been alert to anyone following him and he would have spotted us long before reaching Canano. We would have to figure out another way to find Canano.

Immediately after the call between Ahmed and Canano, Canano called the Engineer in Mexico. Canano asked if the Engineer had talked to his "guy," meaning Luis. The Engineer said no. Canano said that his "brother," meaning Ahmed, had just called him and said that he "saw a problem there. That there was an 'accident.'" The word "accident" is the universal code word used by drug traffickers to mean that either someone has been arrested or a seizure by law enforcement has occurred. The Engineer said, "Don't fuck around." Canano reiterated that he had just received the call from Ahmed. The Engineer said that he would call "over there."

About eight minutes later, Canano called the Engineer again and asked, "Did you get in touch with him?" The Engineer said no, which was not surprising since Luis was no longer in a position to take phone calls. Canano said that he was going "to shut off this phone." The Engineer asked, "How did your guy know that he had an 'accident?'" Canano answered, "He saw it."

And that would be the last call we intercepted over Canano's phone.

With the brothers Luis and Aaron in custody, as well as the 21 kilograms of cocaine, we turned our attention to getting a search warrant for the house on Harrison. Since the cocaine had obviously come from inside that house, we had the probable cause to obtain one. While the affidavit was being prepared, we kept an eye on the house to ensure that no one came or went. No one did. Once the warrant was signed by a judge, we entered the house.

There were no other people inside the house when we entered. Like most stash houses, the residence was sparsely furnished. We discovered 178 kilograms of cocaine hidden in the attic. In one of the empty bedrooms, an agent noticed that the floorboards were loose and the wooden baseboards had been removed. Upon lifting some of the floorboards, he found another 339 kilograms hidden in the vacant space beneath the floor, bringing the total seizure to 517 kilograms. So, the Engineer had not been exaggerating when he had told Canano that there were "500" kilos available in Chicago.

While we did not have probable cause for a search warrant at the house on Colombia, Luis, who lived there, consented to a search of it. We recovered another kilogram of cocaine and $12,000 in cash. We also found a drug ledger which detailed the distribution of over 400 kilograms of cocaine to more than a dozen different customers of the Engineer's organization.

After his arrest, Luis admitted that he was on his way to deliver the 21 kilograms when he was stopped. He said that he was delivering the cocaine on the orders of a man in Mexico who he did not know. Luis said that the man in Mexico would call his cell phone and give him orders about deliveries. It is entirely possible that Luis did not know the identity of the Engineer since Luis had likely been hired locally by Ricardo, the man in charge of the drug distribution group in Chicago. He would have no reason to know the Engineer's identity.

Luis said that he and his brother, Aaron, had constructed the hidden compartment under the floor at the house on

Harrison. He said that they were being paid $5,000 a month to make cocaine deliveries to various customers of the Engineer's organization, none of whom he knew, including Canano and Ahmed. Canano and Ahmed also did not know the identity of Luis, which can be inferred from the fact that they both referred to Luis in phone calls as "the guy" since they did not know his name.

Luis said he never handled any drug money, which was also true. The drug money was handled by the Accountant and his group, people that Luis and Aaron had no reason to know.

State charges were filed against Luis and Aaron and they would remain in state custody until we filed federal charges several months later.

Since Darrell didn't receive his order of 21 kilograms, the money he had fronted was returned to him by Ahmed. We would learn that fact at the end of the investigation.

Chapter 7

The wiretap order for Alonso's phone expired on September 18 and we did not obtain a renewal order. Since the seizure of $80,000 from the money group on September 11, it appeared that Alonso and the others had been removed from their role collecting drug money so there was no reason to maintain the wiretap. It's not unusual for a drug trafficking organization to replace its drug or money crew members with new people following a law enforcement seizure. It's a standard precaution that must be taken to prevent further losses of money or cocaine.

With Canano's phone down as well, we were in the dark as to what was occurring in Chicago. With the seizure of 539 kilograms on September 15 from two members of the drug distribution group, it was likely that the Engineer would be replacing Ricardo and anyone else in his group as well. We would have to rely on the Colorado Springs wiretap of Lazaro's phone to know for sure. It wouldn't be long before we learned that our hunch was correct.

On October 5, agents in Colorado Springs intercepted calls which revealed that Lazaro would be travelling to Chicago to pick up drug money from a man whose nickname was "El Negro." "El Negro" was apparently the replacement for the Accountant and his money crew in Chicago.

On the morning of October 6, we watched Lazaro meet with El Negro and another Hispanic male at a McDonalds restaurant on Cicero Avenue in Chicago. The two men removed two duffel bags and a backpack from their vehicle which probably contained about a million dollars in cash and placed them inside Lazaro's car. After transferring the bags, all three men talked for a few minutes and then went their separate ways.

A couple of agents followed Lazaro and watched him enter the southbound lanes of Interstate 55, on his way back to Colorado. The rest of our surveillance team followed El Negro and his associate to an apartment building on Lawndale Avenue in Chicago.

Since El Negro appeared to be the new money group supervisor in Chicago, we began writing the affidavit to tap his phone. As with the Accountant's phone, we expected to intercept cocaine customers as well as a new drug group supervisor if Ricardo had been replaced, as we suspected he had.

Less than two weeks later, on October 17, Lazaro returned to Chicago to take delivery of more drug money from El Negro. We watched El Negro meet Lazaro in the parking lot of a Best Buy electronics store in Chicago. El Negro removed three large black duffel bags and placed them into Lazaro's car. After making the exchange, Lazaro headed back to Colorado and El Negro returned to his apartment building on Lawndale.

A few days after this delivery, we discovered that El Negro had vacated his apartment. He was, evidently, no longer part of the money group. It appeared that he had been replaced for unknown reasons. We now had no idea who was handling drug or money deliveries for the Engineer in Chicago.

On November 18, we obtained court authorization to intercept a new cellular phone which we had discovered Canano was using. Since September 15, when he had dropped his phone following our seizure of the 539 kilograms, we had been unaware of any of his activities. We still weren't sure who he was or where he lived. We knew his associate, Ahmed, worked at a furniture store on the north side of Chicago and we would watch that location because we suspected Canano worked there, too. But we were still unable to determine his identity. We knew the identity of one of his customers, Marco, but the other customer, Darrell, remained unidentified.

While we hoped to identify Canano during the wiretap of his new phone, we had only about two weeks to do so. With several other DEA offices involved in this investigation, a nationwide arrest date had been set for December 4, 2003. We were preparing charges for the Chicago-based drug and money group members as well as Canano and his customer group. Our affidavit for the criminal complaint was almost complete. We needed only Canano's real name.

On November 20, at around 5:30 P.M., we intercepted a call between Canano and the customer Darrell. They agreed to meet at a Wendy's restaurant at "Roosevelt and Harlem," in Oak Park.

One of our agents wasn't too far from that Wendy's and he was able to get there in time to watch the meeting. Sitting at a table inside the restaurant were Canano, another Hispanic male, and Darrell. The unknown Hispanic male, we would later learn, was called "Alamo" and he had arrived in Chicago in October to oversee drug distribution for the Engineer. He had replaced Ricardo, who had left Chicago sometime after the seizure of the 500 kilograms in Aurora. Once they were done eating, the agent watched the men leave the restaurant and get into their respective vehicles. The license plate on Darrell's car was registered in his name at his residence in south suburban Romeoville. The plate on Canano's car was also registered in his true name at his residence in Elmwood Park, a suburb west of Chicago. We now knew who he was, and his name was inserted into the criminal complaint.

Around this same time, the anonymous source in Mexico sent another e-mail to the Illinois State trooper. The source claimed that the Engineer's associates in Mexico were sending cocaine to Chicago in buses. Since we had stopped a tour bus in July and seized almost $300,000 in drug money, it was probable that this claim was true. The source also wrote that a suburban police officer in Chicago had obtained a warehouse and was helping unload these buses when they arrived. The source added that the officer was of Mexican ancestry but spoke English like he was of Italian origin. That language description fit Canano to a tee. When Canano spoke to Darrell or Marco, he spoke English like a Hollywood mob guy. By this time, we had confirmed that Canano worked at the furniture store on Grand Avenue and it had never appeared to us that he had any affiliation with law enforcement.

Over the next several days, we intercepted several calls between Canano and Darrell discussing the order of 21 kilograms of cocaine for $18,500 per kilogram. In one of the calls, Canano told Darrell that there were 100 kilograms available to be purchased. But Darrell would eventually cancel his order.

On November 24, Canano called Darrell and Darrell told him, "This dude, man, he went to the 'store' already," which meant that the person to whom Darrell was going to sell Canano's kilograms had already gotten them from someone else. After Canano complained, Darrell said that his guy would purchase more cocaine in a few days. Canano said, "Whatever I can keep for him, I'll keep for him," which meant that Canano would try to hold some kilograms in reserve for Darrell's buyer. Canano continued, "But this motherfucker here, he went and built a deck already for '200 square feet.' In two days, man. He's already asking to borrow my 'workers.'" What Canano was saying was that one of his associates, who we later learned was the new drug group supervisor named Alamo, had distributed 200 kilograms ("200 square feet") in two days and he wanted access to the 100 kilograms that had been reserved for Canano ("he's already asking to borrow my 'workers'"). Canano and Darrell agreed to talk a few days later should Darrell's buyer need more cocaine.

Canano and Darrell, however, were running out of time. On December 3, we obtained the arrest and search warrants for the drug and money crews operating in Chicago, as well as for Canano and the members of his customer group. We made the decision to arrest Canano and Darrell on the night of December 3, a day before the scheduled nationwide arrests. We had search warrants for Canano's furniture store and his house in Elmwood Park. Our hope was that either Canano or Darrell would cooperate and help us identify the new members of the drug and money crews who had replaced Ricardo and the Accountant.

We arrested Canano at his furniture store at about 8:00 at night. As I was patting him down, I felt a hard object in an inside pocket of his jacket. The hard object was a police badge and identification card that had been issued by a small suburban police department. When I asked him about it, he blurted out, "I'm a cop." For a split second I thought we had the wrong guy, but then I remembered the e-mail from the anonymous source in Mexico. Whoever the source was, his information was spot on. Canano was a part-time auxiliary police officer with a small suburban department and he had, in fact, been helping the new supervisor (Alamo) of the cocaine distribution group in Chicago as the anonymous source had said. We would later learn that Alamo and Canano had taken delivery of 289 kilograms of cocaine in late November that had been concealed in a tour bus.

Canano would not cooperate with us and our search of his furniture store was fruitless. A concurrent search of his house, however, resulted in the seizure of $31,365 in cash and two handguns.

Around the same time we took Canano into custody, his customer Darrell was arrested as he pulled into the driveway of his residence in Romeoville. Inside his car agents found a nine-millimeter handgun and a backpack with $24,000 in cash. We found nothing of significance inside his house.

We locked up both Darrell and Canano that night and prepared for the next day's arrests.

On December 4, a team of agents arrested Gerardo at the apartment in Melrose Park. Alonso and Toucan were not present as they had returned to Mexico some days earlier. There was no drug money found inside the apartment, which was not surprising since they had not been involved in collecting money since mid-September when their apartment had been searched by police.

Ahmed was arrested at his house in Round Lake Beach. He, too, had no contraband at his house.

After Canano's customer, Marco, was taken into custody, a search of his residence in South Holland resulted in the seizure of $89,175 in cash and three handguns. A search of a safe deposit box that Marco had rented at a local bank was also conducted. The box contained $498,500 in cash.

We also searched a safe deposit box that Canano's other customer, Darrell, had rented. That box contained $20,000 in cash. We also seized, with the assistance of the IRS, one of his bank accounts which contained $29,880.

We looked for the Accountant and Ricardo at their last known address, an apartment building in suburban Bensenville. However, their apartments had been vacated months earlier when they were replaced by El Negro and Alamo, whose identity and role in the organization we had yet to determine.

We also could not find Ruben, the original member of the Accountant's money crew who had quit the organization sometime in June of 2003. He would remain a fugitive until June 14, 2004, when he was taken into custody in Kansas City, Kansas.

The brothers Luis and Aaron, the previous drug distribution group members under Ricardo, had remained in custody since their arrest on September 15. They would be transferred to federal custody and the state charges would be dropped.

Two weeks after we arrested Canano, the Chicago Tribune reported that he had been fired from the police department.

Chapter 8

We spent the last weeks of December, 2003, conducting interviews and gathering additional evidence. With the arrest of Canano and the others, it was likely that Alamo, who had been in charge of drug distribution after Ricardo left, had been replaced. It was also likely that a new group of people were now responsible for collecting drug money.

In fact, a new group of individuals had already taken over drug distribution and money collection in Chicago for the Engineer. They took over at the beginning of 2004, perhaps a month after our round-up.

This new crew, we learned, was headed by a man nicknamed "Tupo." Tupo oversaw the members of both the drug and money groups. We conducted a few more wiretaps of his group and our surveillance efforts throughout January and February of 2004 led to the identification of two residences on the south side of Chicago, both of which we believed to be stash houses; one for drug money and the other for cocaine.

On February 23, 2004, we obtained search warrants for both houses. We planned to serve the warrants simultaneously at 4 o'clock that afternoon.

My team approached the first house, in the 4400 block of South Karlov in Chicago, and after not receiving an answer to our knocks, we breached the door and made entry. After searching the house and finding no one inside, we noticed that the television in the living room was on. A video game system was attached to the television and there was a video game in "paused" mode on the screen. We soon learned that the lone resident of the house had seen us coming and had fled out the back door. He was caught by the agents who were covering the rear of the house. Prior to fleeing, however, he had evidently paused his video game perhaps hoping he could return to it once we had completed our raid.

We searched the house – which, again, was sparsely furnished like most stash houses - and found 13 duffel bags and a cardboard box in one of the bedrooms. There was a total of 330 kilograms of cocaine inside the bags and the box.

In the meantime, another team of agents were executing the warrant at the money stash house in the 6300 block of South Kildare. As with our team, they received no answer to their knocks on the front door and had to make a forcible entry into the residence. Two men who had been working in the garage of the residence jumped a fence and tried to get away. Both were taken into custody. The men had been in the garage creating a trap compartment in a vehicle. Agents found two duffel bags in the garage, which contained a total of approximately $575,000 in cash. Some or all that money was going to be placed inside the compartment that the men had been constructing.

During a search of the house, agents discovered multiple surveillance cameras around the perimeter of the house. All the cameras could be monitored from the basement of the house. The cameras may have been used for two purposes: to get warning of a police raid and to keep an eye on their vehicles which were parked on the street in front of the house. During a search of one of those vehicles that was parked in front, agents found six more kilograms of cocaine.

We took four men into custody from the two houses, along with a total of 336 kilograms of cocaine and $575,000 in cash. All four men would plead guilty to various drug conspiracy charges the following year. The man arrested at the cocaine stash house admitted to being hired to guard the cocaine. He said he was paid $1,000 a week for his services.

The man in charge of this group, Tupo, could not be found. He remains a fugitive today.

The day after our raids, February 24, the authorities in Mexico arrested the Engineer in Mexico City. He would remain in custody until he was extradited to the United States in January of 2007 to face charges in U.S. District Court in the District of Colorado, where this case originally began.

In April of 2004, we indicted the Doctor, who was Canano's backer in Mexico, after we determined his identity and learned that he was now living in the Chicago area. We took him into custody at his residence in a northwest suburb of Chicago.

It was around this time that we learned the identity and role of Alamo, the man who had replaced Ricardo overseeing cocaine deliveries in Chicago. We indicted him in May and took him into custody shortly afterwards.

In the summer of 2004, we conducted an additional wiretap of another of the Engineer's customers in Chicago. The customer's name was Raul and we had hoped that tapping his phone might lead us to people who may have taken over for the Engineer or his drug and money crews in Chicago. It didn't pan out the way we hoped; we ended up charging Raul and two associates following the seizure of just one kilogram of cocaine. All three would plead guilty or be convicted at trial the following year.

Throughout 2005, most of the people associated with the Engineer pled guilty to assorted drug conspiracy charges. The customer Darrell pled guilty on June 16, 2005. He would be sentenced the following year to 135 months in prison.

The drug crew member Luis pled guilty on July 6. He would be sentenced to 135 months in prison. His brother, Aaron, also a member of the drug distribution group, pled guilty a week later. He would also be sentenced to 135 months in prison.

Gerardo, a member of the Accountant's money crew, would plead guilty on July 12. He received 135 months in prison. Two days later, Canano pled guilty. He would be sentenced to 160 months in prison. His associate, Ahmed, pled guilty on August 2. He received 90 months in prison.

On September 16, the money crew member Ruben pled guilty. He admitted to delivering 4.4 million dollars in cash to the Engineer's couriers in May and June of 2003. He would be sentenced to 121 months in prison.

Alamo was the last to plead guilty, on September 19. He would be sentenced to 46 months in prison. In his plea agreement, he admitted that he was paid $125 for every kilogram he delivered to the Engineer's customers in Chicago. He also admitted to distributing 289 kilograms of cocaine in November of 2003.

Marco and the Doctor opted to go to trial, which began on September 21. They would both be found guilty by a jury in U.S. District Court in the Northern District of Illinois on October 3. The Doctor would be sentenced on May 9, 2006, to 324 months in prison, a sentence that would later be reduced to 262 months on March 4, 2015. Marco was sentenced on June 16, 2006, to 360 months in prison. The lengthiness of Marco's sentence was partially based on his previous criminal record, which was extensive.

In January of 2007, the Engineer was extradited from Mexico to the District of Colorado. In a news story about the investigation of the Engineer, the Colorado Springs Gazette reported in October of 2004 that one of his couriers had transported 43 million dollars in drug money in one year's time. The majority of that money had come out of Chicago.

The Engineer would plead guilty in U.S. District Court in Colorado on October 17, 2008. He was sentenced on February 18, 2009, to 180 months in prison.

During the investigation, we had seized 876 kilograms of cocaine and approximately 1.6 million dollars in Chicago. Twenty-one individuals were charged and ultimately convicted. Four people remain fugitives.

Part Two

Chapter 1

In the early 2000's, a drug cartel group in Mexico which called itself "La Empresa" (Spanish for "the Company") was headed by a man named Carlos Rosales-Mendoza. The group operated in the Mexican state of Michoacan, which is in southwestern Mexico on the Pacific coast. They were aligned with the Gulf Cartel and that cartel's armed wing of enforcers, "the Zetas." The Zetas were a group of Mexican Army Special Forces soldiers who had been enticed to leave the army and work for the cartel.

In October of 2004, Rosales-Mendoza was arrested by Mexican police. Following his arrest, a man named Nazario "el Chayo" Moreno-Gonzalez took control of the cartel. Moreno-Gonzalez was also nicknamed "El Mas Loco" ("The Craziest One"). Moreno was born in Apatzingan, Michoacan, in 1970 and he reportedly earned his second nickname because of his violent behavior as a child. Sometime after taking control of La Empresa, Moreno began pushing Zeta associates out of Michoacan. La Empresa was renamed "La Familia Michoacana" or "La Familia" (Spanish for "the family") for short. The group announced their existence in September of 2006 after dumping five severed human heads onto the dance floor of a night club in the city of Uruapan in Michoacan. A note was left with the severed heads which read, "The family doesn't kill for money. It doesn't kill women. It doesn't kill innocent people, only those who deserve to die. Know that this is divine justice."

Moreno ran the La Familia cartel as a quasi-religious cult, issuing "spiritual manuals" to members of the organization. Those manuals contained his own pseudo-Christian writings about self-improvement. Some members of the cartel were required to attend training camps in Michoacan where they would receive both bible lessons and military-type training.

Other top leaders of the cartel group included Jose "el Chango" ("the monkey") Mendez-Vargas, who was considered second-in-command to Moreno; Servando "la Tuta" Gomez; Arnold "la Minsa" Rueda-Medina; and Enrique Plancarte-Solis. By the end of February, 2015, all of these men, as well as Moreno, would either be dead or in a Mexican prison.

In addition to Chicago, the city of Atlanta also serves as a major drug trafficking hub for most of the same cartels. And like most cartels, La Familia established a presence in both Atlanta and Chicago at least as early as 2006 or 2007. An investigation conducted by DEA agents in Atlanta in 2007 of a La Familia group led to the investigation in Chicago.

Most of the phones we tapped during this investigation were pre-paid, Nextel Direct Connect, or "Push-To-Talk," phones, which were a popular form of communication for drug traffickers during that time. The phones could be obtained by drug traffickers without requiring them to provide any personal identification. If there was any subscriber information associated with the phone it was usually a false name and a non-existent address. We would eventually tap 49 phones before completing the first phase of the investigation.

The DEA group in Chicago that conducted this investigation consisted of one supervisor, ten DEA Special Agents, and three police officers. I was part of that group as were my partners, Special Agent Luke McConnell and TFO Nick Stull. The three police officers assigned to our group were from the Chicago, Aurora, and Arlington Heights Police Departments.

The Assistant U.S. Attorneys ("AUSA") who did the bulk of the work writing the wiretap applications and orders, as well as overseeing the prosecution of the defendants, were Amar Bhachu, Michael Donovan, Stephen Baker, Megan Church and Erika Csicsila.

As I mentioned earlier, this case was the result of an investigation begun by the DEA office in Atlanta, Georgia, of a La Familia group operating in the Atlanta area beginning in 2007. This section tells the story of the investigation of the La Familia cartel's drug trafficking activities in Chicago from 2007 through 2010.

Chapter 2

In July of 2007, the DEA office in Atlanta, Georgia, was investigating the La Familia cartel operatives in their city. They began intercepting telephone calls made by an individual whose role in the organization was unclear at the time. During one of the calls, this individual – who I will refer to as "Felix" - arranged to meet with a person who was nicknamed "Manolo." Manolo would be the first cocaine customer of La Familia who we encountered in Chicago. After discussing where they would meet, Manolo told Felix that he was driving a black Jeep, a detail that would help us find and identify him later. Although this meeting was not surveilled by us, the phone calls made clear that Manolo was a customer living somewhere in the Chicago area.

On August 6, 2007, Felix received a call from Manolo who asked if the "new machines" had arrived. The word "machines" was the code for kilograms of cocaine. Felix asked Manolo how many "machines" he needed. Manolo replied, "Fifteen." Felix said that the fifteen kilograms could probably be delivered to Manolo that same day. Over the next two hours, Manolo cancelled his order for fifteen kilograms and subsequently requested a "hand," which meant that he now only wanted five kilograms. The word "hand" is commonly used by drug traffickers as a code word to mean a quantity of five. An hour later, Felix called and told Manolo that "the guy" was around the corner. The reference to "the guy" meant that a courier from the drug distribution group was near Manolo's residence with the five kilograms of cocaine. The calls indicated that

Manolo would meet this courier at a parking lot not far from Manolo's house.

A team of agents was able to find a person believed to be Manolo sitting in a black Jeep in a parking lot in the western suburb of North Riverside, exactly where he had told Felix he would be. Manolo then met with the driver of a red Ford F-150, who we believed was Felix's courier. It was likely that the man in the Ford was delivering five kilograms of cocaine to Manolo during this meeting, but no exchange was actually seen by us. After the meeting, Manolo drove his Jeep to a house in the neighboring suburb of Broadview, a house we would later confirm was Manolo's residence. The Ford truck also drove away, and surveillance agents followed it to a residence in the 700 block of Shannon Drive in Romeoville, a suburb southwest of Chicago. Based on those intercepted calls in Atlanta, we believed this house was a location used by La Familia's drug distribution group as a stash house to store cocaine. Additional surveillance of the residence would be necessary to confirm that suspicion, but it was the first residence we identified that we suspected was occupied by La Familia workers.

The next morning, August 7, agents were watching the Shannon Drive residence when they observed a Hispanic male leave in the same red Ford F-150 that was observed the day before during the meeting with Manolo. Agents followed the man to a Best Buy parking lot in Riverside. The man parked his truck in the lot and walked into the store. He would never come back to the vehicle.

Surveillance agents could not find the man inside the Best Buy or anywhere else in the immediate area. After watching the truck around the clock for almost 30 hours, it became obvious that the man had spotted surveillance and had abandoned the vehicle in the lot. A drug-sniffing dog was brought to the vehicle and the dog alerted to the scent of drugs coming from inside. We suspected the driver would not return to the truck, so we decided to have the vehicle towed to a local police station where we could conduct a thorough search. At the police station, we discovered the truck had a hydraulically-operated hidden compartment. Once we got the compartment open, we found ten kilograms of cocaine concealed inside.

On August 9, several agents returned to watch the Shannon Drive residence. There was no activity and a gray Acura that had been previously seen at the residence was no longer parked in the driveway. It was apparent that the house had been abandoned. Since the drug courier in the Ford F-150 had spotted surveillance agents the previous day, the members of the distribution group took the precaution of abandoning the house that they assumed was probably known to law enforcement. They had vacated the house while we were tied up watching the Ford truck at the Best Buy parking lot.

But where they had gone and finding them again would not be easy. We had no identifying information for the person who had abandoned the F-150. We also did not know the identity of any other individuals who may have lived at the Shannon Drive residence. The license plates of both the F-150 and the gray Acura were registered to names and addresses that turned out to be dead-end leads, a not uncommon occurrence. Vehicles that are used by members of either the drug or money groups are rarely registered in their names or at their actual residences. In some cases, the vehicles are registered to false names and non-existent addresses. In other cases, the vehicles are registered in the names of real people, but they are persons who are not involved with any drug trafficking activity and are merely known associates or friends of the traffickers. In either case, the license plate information that we had was not going to lead us to the location where the drug group had moved.

Because drug groups usually rent houses and do not buy them, we considered approaching the owner of the Shannon Drive residence to obtain the rental information of the occupants. But since we did not know the potential relationship between the owner and the occupants, we decided against it.

Furthermore, it was likely that whoever had rented the house had done so at the behest of the drug group and was probably not the person who was actually living at the house or working for the group. So, the rental information was likely to be a dead-end lead as well.

The only option at that point was to conduct surveillances of Manolo's residence in Broadview. Since Manolo was a customer being served by the drug distribution group, following him was the best way to find the group's new residence. It would also be possible to find the group responsible for collecting drug payments, whose identities and locations we had not discovered up to this point. We would spend several days watching Manolo's house throughout the last few weeks of August and into September.

On September 5, 2007, surveillance of Manolo's house paid off. Agents observed a purple Chevy Tahoe parked in front of the house. It was a vehicle that had not been seen at Manolo's house during previous surveillances. We watched two Hispanic males walk out of Manolo's house, enter the Tahoe, and drive away. The vehicle was followed to a residence in the 100 block of Kingston Road in Bolingbrook, a suburb southwest of Chicago. Parked in the driveway was the same gray Acura that had been observed at the Shannon Drive residence. We suspected this was the new residence where the drug distribution group had moved after abandoning the house on Shannon Drive.

Surveillance of this residence began immediately. Sometime in late October or early November, however, this house was also abandoned. Again, no agents had been on surveillance when the occupants left so no one knew when or why the residence had been vacated. It was possible that agents had been spotted watching the house and the occupants took the necessary step of moving again. We had no way of knowing for sure. It was clear, though, that this group would change locations as frequently as they felt necessary.

In early November, we made the decision to contact the owner/landlord of the Kingston residence. He told us that he had not received the rent payment for November. He gave us the name of the individual who had rented the house, a name which meant nothing to us. The landlord said that he had received a phone call from an unknown individual who informed him that the house would be vacated by November 11, and that a final rent payment would be delivered to the landlord before that day. The landlord had made arrangements to meet with this unknown person and collect the rent. We decided to surveil this meeting to see who would show up to make the payment.

On November 8, we watched a Hispanic male meet with the landlord and deliver the final rent payment for the Kingston residence. This time, the license plates of the vehicle were registered in the man's name, as well as his correct address, so we were able to properly identify him. We would later learn that this man had no drug trafficking role with the drug group we were investigating. He had merely been sent to make the payment so that no one from the actual drug group would have to do it. It was a smart move on their part. They obviously suspected that law enforcement was onto them and if they sent a member of their group, that member could lead us to them again. So, they sent an acquaintance they could trust and who did not work for them. We would spend a lot of time surveilling this man, however, before we learned that, and those numerous surveillances would lead us nowhere.

We would also learn from the landlord that a real estate agent named Maria had helped facilitate the rental of the Kingston house by the occupants. I knew the agent from a previous investigation and I was aware of her association with drug traffickers from Michoacan, Mexico. We would see her again in the future.

The landlord told us we could search the house after he confirmed it had been vacated. On November 12, we searched the residence, with the consent of the landlord, and confirmed that the house had been abandoned. But the occupants had left behind some useful leads. Perhaps they had felt they had to abandon the house quickly and did not have the time to remove everything that would be of interest to us. Whatever the reason, they left behind 125 plastic wrappings consistent in size and shape with wrappings used to package kilograms of cocaine. More importantly, they also left behind a drug ledger which contained a list of customer names and nicknames. As with all groups responsible for distributing cocaine, this ledger was maintained to keep track of the number of kilograms that had been fronted to each individual customer.

We were also incredibly fortunate in recovering a list of phone numbers belonging to some of the same customers named in the drug ledger. The list of phone numbers was hidden under a cable box located on top of an entertainment center. The phone numbers were contained on a single sheet of paper with the pre-printed words "Grocery List" at the top of the page. The nicknames written next to the phone numbers matched neatly with the nicknames recorded in the drug ledger. It was a huge mistake on the part of the drug group members to leave that phone list behind. We could use those numbers to help identify the customers named in the ledger and we could also use the historical calling activity to find their new phones.

A closer review of the ledger revealed that this drug group had delivered over 2,000 kilograms of cocaine in a six-week period from June through August of 2007, which is a substantial amount of cocaine in such a short period of time. All that cocaine was likely distributed to customers in the greater Chicago area. The ledger confirmed that "Manolo," as it was printed in the ledger, had received five kilograms of cocaine on August 6, the original delivery intercepted during the Atlanta wire that had started our investigation in Chicago.

Other customers recorded in the ledger included someone named "Ponciano," who had received 187 kilograms of cocaine between June 18 and August 7, 2007. Another individual named "Carlos" had received 190 kilograms of cocaine between June 24 and August 7. We had no idea who Ponciano and Carlos were, but we now had their phone numbers. Even though those phones were going to be changed, analyzing the telephone calling records was likely to lead us not only to Ponciano, Carlos, and the other customers named in the ledger, but also to the individuals responsible for distributing cocaine to them. And there still had to be another group of individuals responsible for collecting the drug payments. We had no idea who those people were or where they lived. The phone records would be crucial in the next stage of the investigation.

As 2007 ended, McConnell sent out subpoenas for the phone records of the cellular phone numbers we had discovered at the Kingston residence. Almost all the phone numbers that were written on the "Grocery List" had been deactivated within days of our search, which was not surprising. However, the calling records of each individual phone would provide us with the opportunity to identify currently active phones of both the drug distribution members and the locally-based customers. It would take a lot of time and effort to wade through all the records we were receiving. The sheer volume of the records made the task infinitely more difficult.

Another factor that complicates the analysis of these phone records is the pace at which the records arrive. Some phone companies respond to subpoenas more quickly than others so there are times when a potentially good phone number is identified, we learn that is has already been active for several weeks meaning that it is not likely to be in use for much longer. Drug traffickers know they need to switch their phones frequently, so it is not unusual to discover a number after a trafficker has already discarded it and moved on to another one. It's a frustrating, and frequent, occurrence.

Chapter 3

As the phone records came in from the various cell phone companies, McConnell identified a phone number that looked to be associated with the individuals who had abandoned the Kingston stash house. He was right. In March of 2008, McConnell and AUSA Bhachu obtained a court order which allowed us to use cellular location technology - the activity commonly called "pinging" - to find the actual physical location of the phone. On March 11, the phone was "pinged" to a residence in the 8300 block of Sayre Avenue in Burbank, a suburb south of Chicago. When an agent drove by the residence, he observed the same purple Chevy Tahoe that used to be at the Kingston stash house. The Sayre Avenue residence was a new location for what we thought would be members of the drug distribution group.

We did not have probable cause to obtain court authorization to tap the cell phone found at the Sayre Avenue residence. The phone didn't stay in use long enough, anyway. But we had a physical location to watch while we continued to analyze phone records looking for Carlos, Ponciano, and the other customers listed in the ledger. We knew we needed to be more cautious when watching this house since our previous surveillance efforts had already caused the abandonment of two potential stash locations.

In addition to our physical surveillances, we also conducted what is called "trash pulls." Looking through the trash of drug dealers can sometimes result in obtaining useful information, such as phone numbers, drug ledgers, or other evidence of drug trafficking. On the morning of the scheduled garbage collection day, we would retrieve whatever trash was placed at the curb by the occupants of the Sayre residence. We approached a friendly garbage man and he would pick up the trash during his route down the street and keep the trash from the Sayre residence separate from the trash of the neighbors. We would then meet him at the end of the block and place the Sayre residence trash bags in our vehicles. We would then search through that trash at a nearby police station.

We did these trash pulls at the Sayre residence every week in April and May of 2008. These trash searches are not as glamorous as they may sound. In addition to wading through discarded food items and rotting meat, we also had to deal with several wadded-up lumps of used toilet paper containing fecal matter. McConnell told me that in certain parts of Mexico, the plumbing systems cannot handle toilet paper, so the residents of those areas throw their used toilet paper in the garbage can instead of the toilet. I guess that toilet paper in the trash could be considered solid evidence that whoever the occupants of the Sayre residence were, they had come from one of those areas in Mexico with poor plumbing systems.

During one of our trash searches, an unsuspecting agent came across some of the discarded toilet paper which so disgusted him that he spent the rest of the morning dry-heaving. He was unable to continue searching the trash with us, leaving an amused McConnell and me to finish it ourselves.

As disgusting as the searches could be, they did result in the recovery of some useful information. We recovered several empty cellular phone boxes which helped in identifying new phone numbers. We also discovered heat-sealed plastic bags and a lot of broken and discarded rubber bands. The plastic bags and the rubber bands were good signs to us that drug money was being collected, and possibly stored, at the Sayre residence. We had initially assumed that the Sayre residence was a new cocaine stash house because of the presence of the Chevy

Tahoe, which had been used by members of the drug distribution group at the Kingston house. The stuff we were finding in the trash, however, led us to believe that the Sayre house was more likely being used by the money crew, the group that we had not yet encountered. It is not unusual for a cartel's drug and money groups to exchange vehicles or other organizational assets that are necessary for both the delivery of cocaine and the collection of drug money. Based on the results of our trash searches, we believed we were onto the money group of the organization, which now meant that we did not have any locations identified for the drug distribution group.

In addition to the trash searches, we also conducted sporadic surveillances of the Sayre residence. We counted at least three Hispanic males and one female who appeared to live at the house. On some occasions, we would follow the males when they left the house to identify other associates and residences. In mid-April, we identified a house in the 8400 block of Lockwood Avenue in Burbank, as well as another house in the 8700 block of 55th Avenue in Oak Lawn. But we didn't know the significance of either of those locations. Were they cocaine customers, drug trafficking associates, or simply innocent family members related to the occupants of the Sayre residence? We would have to spend time watching all three residences to determine their importance.

On April 30, 2008, we were conducting surveillance of the 55th Avenue residence in Oak Lawn. We saw a man, a woman, and a child leave the house in a Toyota Solara. We followed the car to a K-Mart parking lot on Pulaski Road in Chicago. After parking in the lot, the male driver met with the driver of a black Ford pick-up truck that was already parked in the lot. The two men talked for a short period of time before returning to their vehicles. The Ford truck contained two other men, so we decided to stop following the Solara and begin following the truck with the three men, which would later prove to be the right decision.

We followed them to the parking lot of a McDonald's restaurant at 84th Street and Pulaski Road in Chicago. All three men went inside and sat at a table. A short time later, two of the men walked out of the McDonalds and met with another man who had just arrived in the parking lot in a Pontiac coupe. After a short conversation, the man from the Pontiac got into the driver's side of the Ford pick-up truck and drove out of the lot. The three men, who had arrived at the McDonalds in the Ford truck, now got into the Pontiac that had just arrived. We split our surveillance team, with some agents following the Ford and the remainder of the team following the Pontiac.

The team of agents following the Ford truck watched it arrive at the residence in the 8400 block of Lockwood Street in Burbank, the same house we had identified during our prior surveillances of the men at the Sayre residence. The vehicle drove into the garage and the overhead door closed behind it. Another car, a beat-up Honda, was parked outside in the driveway.

Meanwhile, the agents watching the three men in the Pontiac followed them from the McDonalds to the parking lot of a grocery store at 87th Street and Cicero Avenue in Burbank. All three men got out of the car and walked into the store.

The Ford truck remained inside the garage at the Lockwood residence for approximately twenty-five minutes before the door opened and the vehicle backed out. Agents followed the truck to the same grocery store where the three men were now waiting inside the Pontiac. The Ford truck parked across a parking aisle from the Pontiac. The three men exited the Pontiac and walked over to the Ford, while the driver of the Ford got out. After exchanging car keys, the three men entered their Ford and the lone male returned to his Pontiac. The three men drove out of the lot in the Ford, followed by most of our surveillance team. A handful of agents followed the lone male back to the Lockwood residence. At that point, surveillance of the Lockwood residence was terminated.

The three men in the Ford were followed north on Cicero Avenue. What we had just observed was the standard way that cocaine would be delivered to customers. In stark contrast to the Engineer's drug and money crews who conducted most of their exchanges in the open as described in the first part of this book, most drug traffickers do not like to conduct transactions in public view. Exchanging boxes or duffel bags between vehicles in an open parking lot might draw unwanted attention from the police. So the primary way to minimize public exposure is that a cocaine customer – in this case, the three men with the Ford truck – will provide a vehicle to a drug group's courier – in this case, the man with the Pontiac - who then takes that customer's car to a location where the cocaine is loaded into the vehicle while inside the privacy of a garage. After the cocaine is loaded into the vehicle, the courier returns it to the waiting customers. This delivery method also has the added benefit of not allowing the customer to know the location where the cocaine is stored, which prevents potential robberies. Based on our experience and what we had just observed, we felt confident that the three men's Ford truck now contained cocaine.

Our instincts turned out to be correct. At our request, a Burbank Police officer conducted a traffic stop of the vehicle on Cicero Avenue. The men told officers conflicting stories regarding their travels that day. After a drug-sniffing dog alerted to the odor of drugs emanating from the vehicle, the three men and the truck were transported to the Burbank Police Department for further investigation.

While we were on our way to the police station, we contacted a Chicago Police officer who was an expert at finding hidden trap compartments in vehicles. He came out and discovered a hidden compartment located behind the rear seat of the truck's cab. Inside the compartment were eleven kilograms of cocaine.

None of the three men were willing to be interviewed or give statements regarding the kilograms of cocaine found in their vehicle. All three men were fingerprinted and after determining that there were no outstanding warrants for any of them, they were released to preserve the secrecy of our investigation. Had we charged the men at this point, we would have had to disclose the surveillance efforts that led us to them and that would have exposed our knowledge of some of the organization's members and their stash locations, the houses on 55th Avenue and Lockwood Street. We weren't prepared to do that this early in the investigation, so we released the men with the intention of charging them later.

We now knew that the house on Lockwood was occupied by the cocaine courier and that the garage was used to load cocaine into customer's vehicles. We also had good reason to believe that the house on Sayre in Burbank was where the drug money was counted and stored, based on the results of the trash searches we had conducted.

There was a debate amongst us about getting a search warrant for the Lockwood residence. We knew we had probable cause to obtain a warrant because the eleven kilograms had obviously been loaded inside the house's garage. But getting a warrant presented the same dilemma as charging the men would: we would be required to spell out in an affidavit what we knew about the organization and their locations and we just weren't prepared to do that this early in the investigation. We were still trying to identify the organization's cocaine customers, like Ponciano and Carlos, and McConnell had just identified a good cell phone number for Ponciano. We were very close to receiving authorization to conduct a wiretap of it. We also felt that by leaving the stash house unmolested, we could continue to surveil it and intercept additional cocaine deliveries to other customers in the future.

So, we chose to leave the Lockwood residence alone. We continued to conduct surveillance of that house, as well as the houses on Sayre and 55th Avenue. At the end of April, we learned that the owner/landlord of the Sayre residence was selling the house and had asked the occupants to move out. Our surveillances confirmed that the residents of the Sayre house had all relocated to the house on 55th Avenue, which meant that was probably going to be the new money stash house. In early May, the Sayre house was vacated. We had also followed one of the Sayre residents, a lone male, to a house in south suburban Tinley Park. We did not know the importance of that location at the time, but we would later learn that it was the residence of the leader of the money collection group.

As April ended, we had identified two locations associated with the money group (the suspected money stash house on 55th Avenue and the money group leader's house in Tinley Park) and one location associated with a courier for the drug distribution group – the residence on Lockwood in Burbank. We still had not identified any of the group's customers, besides the three men who we had just arrested with the eleven kilograms of cocaine. We expected that to change as we began tapping Ponciano's cell phone in May.

Chapter 4

In early May of 2008, we received court authorization to intercept phone calls over the cellular phone used by Ponciano. We quickly learned that Ponciano and his brother, who was nicknamed "Compadre," lived in Rockford, Illinois, and that they were supplying kilograms of cocaine to several different customers in Chicago. It appeared that Ponciano and Compadre would coordinate cocaine deliveries to their customers in Chicago without ever leaving the comfort of their homes in Rockford. The calls indicated that they had an associate in Chicago who would handle the delivery of cocaine to customers as well as the collection of money after the cocaine was sold by those same customers. We didn't know it at the time, but the man we thought was Ponciano was actually named "Celso." The name Ponciano was used to refer interchangeably to either brother, Compadre or Celso.

On May 11, we began intercepting calls between Ponciano and Compadre discussing the collection of cash from their various customers. It was apparent that these money collections were occurring in Chicago while one, or both, of the brothers remained in Rockford. At about one o'clock in the afternoon, Ponciano received a call from an unidentified male. The unidentified male said, "They told me you are ready with the 'papers.'" The word "papers" is the universal code word meaning drug money. Ponciano replied, "The guys are going to be there. Let me ask them if they are almost there." The unidentified male told Ponciano to call him "when they are ready."

Based on this call, it was clear to us that the unidentified male was a member of the money collection crew since he had told Ponciano that he was available to pick up the "papers." Immediately after this call was intercepted, Ponciano called his brother, Compadre. Ponciano asked Compadre if the "guys" had arrived. Compadre answered, "Like twenty minutes." The reference to "the guys" meant some of Ponciano and Compadre's customers who were on their way to deliver drug money somewhere in Chicago, money that would in turn be picked up by the unidentified male. A few minutes later, Compadre called Ponciano and said, "Call the guy and tell him that they are there now," which meant that the customers had arrived with their drug money and it was ready to be picked up by the unidentified male.

Ponciano then placed a call to the unidentified male and told him that the "guys are there already." The unidentified male said he was on his way.

About an hour later, Compadre called Ponciano to determine where the unidentified male from the money crew was since he evidently had not arrived to meet Compadre or his associate. Ponciano then called the unidentified male and asked him "Are you almost there?" The unidentified male said that he was close by and provided a somewhat coded reference to his location, which we determined to be near 63rd Street and Pulaski Road in Chicago. Ponciano then called Compadre and passed that information on to him. About five minutes later, the unidentified male called Ponciano and said, "I am here." Ponciano said he would "tell them to open for you right now." Ponciano then called his associate in Chicago and told him that "the guy is there" and to "open up."

Based on those calls, we believed that the unidentified male had picked up the drug cash from Ponciano's associate in Chicago. We also assumed that the unidentified male had picked up the cash from inside a garage somewhere near the area of 63rd Street and Pulaski. The instruction of "open up" that had been given by Ponciano to his associate was an order to open the garage door, so the money collection guy could pull his car into the garage. The reason that drug deliveries are made inside garages outside of public view is the same reason that money deliveries are also made in the same manner.

We now suspected that this unidentified male was the person responsible for collecting drug proceeds on behalf of La Familia. We also knew that this person was one of the individuals who had lived at the Sayre residence because the phone number he was using was one that we had discovered during our garbage searches. It was enough probable cause to seek authorization to intercept phone calls. In addition to that phone, we requested authorization to intercept calls on Compadre's phone, too. McConnell and AUSA Bhachu put together the affidavit for those phones and we received court authorization to tap both phones in mid-May.

The calls revealed that the unidentified male collecting the drug proceeds was referred to as "Flaco" and that he was the supervisor of the money collection group operating in Chicago. The money collection group he was overseeing was comprised of at least two men and one woman, as far as we could tell. Flaco was responsible for picking up money from several other customers besides Ponciano and Compadre. One of those customers was "Carlos," whose name we had seen on the drug ledger recovered at the Kingston stash house. Carlos was obviously still a customer of the organization. On May 20, we intercepted a call from Carlos in which he and Flaco discussed the delivery of drug money. On May 26, we intercepted a call in which Flaco told Carlos that he would take delivery of drug money from Carlos the following day. Flaco and Carlos agreed to meet at "Cermak and Austin," two roads that intersect in the town of Cicero, Illinois. They agreed to meet, as Flaco put it, "at around four, the hour of traffic, you know, the time when everyone gets out of work." The next day, at about 5 o'clock in the afternoon, we watched Flaco arrive at a Walgreen's pharmacy parking lot on Cermak Road in Cicero. We watched a Chevrolet Malibu pull alongside Flaco's Toyota Solara. The Malibu was occupied by two Mexican males, one of whom was Carlos. The Malibu then drove out of the lot, followed by Flaco in his Toyota.

The two vehicles travelled in tandem to the 5600 block of 24th Street in the western suburb of Cicero, where both cars pulled into a garage. The male riding in the Malibu with Carlos closed the garage door. About ten minutes later, the garage door opened and Flaco drove his Toyota out. It was safe to assume that Flaco had just taken delivery of drug money from Carlos inside that garage.

As we were following Flaco away from the garage, he placed a call to Ponciano and said, "I'll be there in about twenty, twenty-five minutes, sir." Ponciano replied, "All right, then. Thank you. I'm here in the 'office.' Call me back when you are close." The word "office" was a code word for a garage. About thirty minutes later, we watched Flaco drive his Toyota into an alley at Homan Avenue and West 61st Place in Chicago. Flaco drove his car into a garage of a residence and the door closed behind him. It was obviously the garage that Ponciano's associate used to make drug and money deliveries since it was just a couple of blocks away from the intersection of 63rd and Pulaski.

Flaco remained inside the garage for about fifteen minutes before the door opened and he drove out. We followed him to another residence before he returned to the house on 55th Avenue in Oak Lawn at around 6:30 P.M., where he drove his Toyota into the garage. Based on our surveillances and the calls we intercepted, we were sure that Flaco had picked up drug money from both Carlos and Ponciano's associate and then taken that money to the house in Oak Lawn where it would be counted, stored and packaged for eventual shipment to Mexico.

Our physical surveillances of Flaco indicated to us that he was picking up money from one or two different customers every day. Any time we watched him drive into a residential garage, we could assume that he was taking delivery of drug money inside. Each time Flaco picked up money from a customer's "office," he would return directly to the house on 55th Avenue in Oak Lawn. It was a clear indication that the Oak Lawn residence was the organization's money stash house. The house was occupied by at least two individuals whose responsibility would be to count the money, package it for shipment and, more importantly, watch over it. We also learned at this time that Flaco was the man who was living at the house in Tinley Park that we had identified during our surveillances of the Sayre residence in April and May.

We knew that Flaco was La Familia's representative in Chicago responsible for collecting and counting drug proceeds from the organization's cocaine customers. What we did not know was the representative responsible for distributing the cocaine ("machines") in Chicago. We would come to learn that through Flaco's phone calls.

In mid-May, we intercepted calls between Ponciano and Compadre which indicated that they wanted to return some cocaine and order more, but they did not have the proper contact number, which is not an uncommon occurrence. Because traffickers change their numbers so frequently, some customers fail to keep up with the current contact number. Compadre called Flaco and asked him for the phone number for the "guy down there." The phrase "down there" is usually a coded reference to Mexico. The guy who Compadre was referring to was Felix, the same person who had made the arrangements for the delivery of five kilograms to Manolo in August of 2007. It was now clear to us that Felix was in charge of overseeing both the distribution of cocaine in Chicago and the collection of drug proceeds. Flaco asked if Compadre meant Felix, to which Compadre responded, "Yeah, or the guy that is here that takes the things, because one is missing an 'onion and a half.'" What Compadre meant was that he wanted either Felix's number or the number to the local drug distribution supervisor ("or the guy that is here"). The reference to one missing "an onion and a half" meant that one of the kilograms was short an ounce and a half and they wanted to return it to the drug group. Flaco said, "I will give you the number for the guy down there instead" and then provided a Mexican telephone number for Compadre to call. The area code for the telephone number was in the Mexican state of Tamaulipas, a state that borders the southernmost tip of Texas.

The next day, Compadre called that Mexican number and spoke to Felix. Compadre said he wanted to talk to "the man that sends the guys to the office to work." It was coded language which meant that Compadre was asking for the phone number for the person responsible for delivering cocaine in Chicago. Felix asked Compadre how many he needed, and Compadre replied, "five," which meant that he wanted five kilograms. Felix said that he would have "the guy" call Compadre to arrange the delivery. An hour later, Compadre called Felix again and Felix confirmed that "they are going to call you in a little while."

On May 18, Ponciano received a call from a person who identified himself as "Choche." Ponciano asked, "What Choche, man?" Choche answered, "From the machines," which was a coded reference that meant Choche was the person in charge of the distribution of cocaine in Chicago. Ponciano wasn't immediately sure who Choche was and he asked, "Are you one of the guys from 'down there?'" Ponciano eventually understood who Choche was and asked him if he remembered where the "office" was. Choche said that he did and told Ponciano that he would send "the guy" the following day. The reference to "the guy" meant Choche's drug runner. Since Choche was in charge, he would not be delivering the cocaine himself. Ponciano agreed to make an exchange of cocaine the following day since Choche said his "guy was busy."

A few minutes after this call was intercepted, Compadre called Flaco and told him, in coded language, that he had wanted to return a kilogram of cocaine that was "defective" but he had been given the wrong phone number. Compadre's reference to the kilogram being "defective" was a reference to the kilogram that was missing an ounce and a half. In instances like that, a "defective" kilogram can be returned in exchange for another one of better quality if the original kilogram has not been tampered with or altered in any way. Compadre complained that he could not get in touch with the person in charge of delivering cocaine in Chicago to make that return. Flaco said, "The guy is far away, if it's Choche." Compadre asked if the person responsible for cocaine deliveries was named "Choche." Flaco said yes. Flaco then provided Compadre with a phone number for Choche, which was a different number than the one we had just intercepted him using when he called Ponciano. Flaco also told Compadre to "change the 'appliance,'" which meant that he wanted Compadre to use a new or different cell phone before calling Choche.

Although we did not need it, we received additional confirmation that Flaco was responsible for money collection and Choche oversaw cocaine deliveries in a phone call between Flaco and a customer who did not have an "office" in the Chicago area. This customer's nickname was "Squert" and he lived in Wisconsin. On May 21, Squert called Flaco and told him he wanted to drop off "papers." While discussing the logistics of delivering the money, Squert asked Flaco about getting more cocaine. Flaco said, "the thing is, I am not the one with the 'machines'...I don't move the 'machines.'" Flaco was telling Squert that he only collected currency and he did not handle any cocaine deliveries.

We now had the nickname of La Familia's head of cocaine distribution in Chicago, as well as the numbers of two cellular telephones that he was using. McConnell and AUSA Bhachu typed up an affidavit for those two phones and we received court authorization to tap them in mid-May. Neither phone, however, would be in use for very long.

The calls we intercepted over Choche's phones provide a good illustration of how the drug distribution group receives instructions from superiors in Mexico concerning the delivery of cocaine to local customers. On Saturday, May 24, we intercepted calls over one of Choche's two phones which indicated that a different customer from Wisconsin, whose name was "Saul," was in Chicago expecting to return one kilogram of cocaine and take delivery of five new ones. At about 11:15 in the morning, Saul called Choche and told him that he was at a Denny's Restaurant on Cicero Avenue in Oak Lawn. Choche told Saul that he would send "the guy" over. Fifteen minutes later, two of our agents watched an unidentified male drive into the parking lot and meet with a man we later determined to be Saul. The unidentified male then got into Saul's Pontiac and drove away. Saul then walked into the Denny's restaurant.

Again, this is the preferred method of making cocaine deliveries to customers. The member of the drug group, in this case the unidentified male who was a runner for Choche, took possession of the customer's car, in this case Saul from Wisconsin, and drove it to the location where the cocaine would be loaded. This method allows the drug group to make deliveries out of public view and also prevents Saul, or any other customer, from knowing where the cocaine is being stored and/or loaded into a vehicle.

The male driving Saul's Pontiac was followed to a garage behind a residence in the 4600 block of West 84th Place in Oak Lawn, a location we had not been aware of. The man drove the car into the garage and closed the overhead door behind him.

At around 11:50 A.M., Saul called Choche and asked him if "they had called." Choche asked, "Who?" Saul said, "From down there," referring to Mexico. Choche said, "No, they haven't called me." Saul said that he would "call over there" and call Choche back. A few minutes later, Saul called Choche and said that he was still waiting to hear from someone in Mexico about the number of kilograms that Saul would be given. Saul told Choche, "They already picked up the car, but they're confirming the 'number' for me right now, over there." Choche said, "Oh, all right, all right."

In this call, Saul was explaining that he was trying to contact his "backer" in Mexico to receive approval to get cocaine. The phrase "they already picked up the car" meant that Saul's vehicle had been taken by the drug courier, which we observed had just occurred at the Denny's parking lot. The phrase "they're confirming the number for me right now," meant that Saul's contacts in Mexico were still determining the number of kilograms that Saul would receive. Choche had also not received any instructions from his superior about the number of kilograms to be delivered to Saul.

Choche, using his second phone, called an unknown male in Mexico. That male asked Choche if he could provide kilograms to Saul. Choche said that he could. The male then called Choche back twenty minutes later and instructed him to give Saul three kilograms of cocaine and not to take back the one that Saul was trying to return. Choche agreed.

Choche then called Saul and told him, in coded language, that he had been instructed to give Saul three kilograms of cocaine and to give back the kilogram that Saul was trying to return. Saul said that he would "call over there right now," meaning that he was going to call his backer in Mexico as he was evidently unhappy with what Choche had told him. This call also made clear that the kilogram that Saul was trying to return was inside his vehicle since Choche had made clear that it was going to be returned to Saul.

At 12:47 P.M., Saul called Choche and asked, "Did they confirm with you?" Choche said, "No, what did they tell you?" Saul said, "That it was five cold Modelos and the hot one that stayed there." What Saul meant was that he had received confirmation from his contact in Mexico that he would receive five kilograms ("five cold Modelos") and the kilogram that he was trying to return ("the hot one that stayed there"). Choche said, "Okay, let me call right now." The reason Choche would have to call his superior again was because his original instructions were to deliver three kilograms and return the one that Saul was trying to exchange. Saul was now saying that he expected to receive five new kilograms in addition to the "defective" one that was going to be returned to him.

Choche then called the same male in Mexico that he had previously spoken to and said, "Listen, this guy is asking me if you have a 'hand,'" which meant five kilograms. The male said, "No, I already talked to his brother and told him: I'm going to lend him three, four, no more. That way the 'hand' would be complete with the one we were going to return." Choche confirmed, "So I should put four, that's all?" The male said yes. Choche said, "Then I give him four and the 'broken one.'" The male said, "Yeah, exactly." Based on this call, it was safe to assume that Saul's "backer" in Mexico was his brother.

At the time these calls were being made, Saul's Pontiac remained inside the garage on 84th Place. The man who had picked up the vehicle from Saul was awaiting instructions as to how many kilograms to load into the car.

Choche then called Saul and told him that he would be getting four kilograms of cocaine and the kilogram that Saul was trying to return. Saul said that was fine. Thirty minutes later, Saul called Choche again and asked if "the cousin" was on his way. The reference to the "cousin" meant the male who had taken Saul's Pontiac from the Denny's parking lot. The word "cousin" does not literally mean a relative but is a Spanish slang word used to mean "dude" or "man." Choche said he would find out where the guy was. A minute later, Saul called Choche and told him, "He's here, cousin, he's here." At the time of that call, agents saw the man driving Saul's Pontiac into the Denny's parking lot. Saul came out of the Denny's, got into his car and drove out of the lot. The man who delivered the Pontiac got back into his car, which he had left in the parking lot after taking Saul's car earlier that morning, and drove away.

The two agents on surveillance that day were unable to follow Saul when he left the restaurant and lost him in traffic. But even though we knew he now had five kilograms of cocaine in his car, it is unlikely that we would have stopped him and seized the cocaine. We were only a day or two into the wiretaps of Choche and conducting a seizure would have resulted in Choche dumping the two phones we were listening to. We needed more time to identify other cocaine customers. And five kilograms, in our view, was not an amount significant enough to justify the risk of losing the wiretaps. It would turn out, however, that the drug transaction with Saul would be the only one we would intercept during the wiretap, as Choche would be changing his phones much sooner than we had anticipated.

By the end of May, we were monitoring a cellular telephone used by Flaco, one used by Ponciano, one used by Compadre, and the two used by Choche. We were still searching the trash from the residence on 55th Avenue in Oak Lawn once a week. We were also keeping watch over that residence, but we rarely observed anything more than Flaco driving his car into and out of the garage. We did observe several individuals who appeared to live at the residence, but Flaco seemed to be the only person who left the house to take delivery of cash from customers.

It was a hectic month and we weren't able to conduct surveillance on all that we would have liked. In addition to the phones we were monitoring in this investigation, we were also tapping phones in another unrelated case which caused significant manpower issues when it came to conducting surveillances. We would occasionally not be able to surveil an event because we were pre-occupied with other activities. In one instance, we were unable to surveil Flaco making a money delivery to a courier who would transport the cash to Mexico.

On May 22, we intercepted a call from a man who identified himself as "Beto's brother-in-law." The man asked Flaco if he was ready. Flaco said that "no one has said anything to me." What Flaco meant was that he had not received any instructions to deliver money to the courier and he was not authorized to make a delivery until he had the approval of his superiors in Mexico, most likely Felix. The courier told Flaco that he could call later "when they give you the okay." The courier's statement meant that he was also aware that Flaco could not make a money delivery without the proper approval. A little over an hour later, Flaco called the courier and told him he had received the approval "to deliver." Flaco said he would call when he was ready.

At 2:30 in the afternoon, Flaco called the courier and told him he was ready. After they agreed to meet at a McDonald's restaurant on the south side of Chicago, Flaco asked, "Who are you? Are you the one from last time?" The courier said, "Yes." Flaco then asked, "Mike?" to which the courier responded, "No." Flaco then said, "You are the one from the van, right?" The courier answered, "Yeah, the van." They then confirmed they would meet at a McDonalds restaurant. We intercepted subsequent calls that indicated that they had, in fact, met at the McDonalds that afternoon. We had not been in any position to surveil the exchange as we were tied up with another activity.

These calls made clear to us that Flaco had delivered money to this courier at the McDonalds restaurant, and that the courier was responsible for transporting that money out of Chicago. Another significant part of the calls was that Flaco was not sure who this courier was, which was an indication that there were other couriers besides this man transporting money for the organization which, as we saw in the Engineer's investigation, is not unusual since most organizations use multiple couriers. Flaco had asked if this courier was "Mike" and when the courier said no, Flaco asked if he was "from the van." The courier then confirmed that he was the one with "the van."

Although we couldn't watch this cash delivery from Flaco to the courier, we now had a telephone number for a money courier who worked for the organization. The number was a cellular telephone which was subscribed in the real name of the courier. His name was "Ismael" and he had a residence in the 5100 block of South Rockwell in Chicago. We also knew that the cartel associate who hired him, or at the very least had vouched for him, was his brother-in-law, "Beto." Like most money couriers, it's likely that Ismael did not know Flaco or anyone else working for La Familia's drug and money crews in Chicago.

As the month of May ended, we had done pretty well identifying cocaine customers, money couriers, and potential stash houses. We felt confident with the way the investigation was progressing.

Things were about to dramatically change.

Chapter 5

On the morning of June 2, 2008, a few agents recovered the trash from the Oak Lawn residence and began searching through it. They found a piece of paper which contained the Spanish word "entrego" handwritten next to the number "1,265,724" with a corresponding date of May 28. The word "entrego" means "delivered" or "delivery," but did it mean that $1,265,724 had been delivered to the Oak Lawn stash house? Or did it mean that the money had been delivered to a courier and was no longer inside the residence? We had no way of knowing for sure. Another page indicated a delivery of "489,255" had been made on May 30, but there was also no way of knowing if that money remained in the house or had been shipped off to Mexico.

While agents were sifting through the garbage, another agent was watching the front of the Oak Lawn residence. At 7:30 A.M., he watched a Cook County Sheriff's deputy park his vehicle in the driveway and walk toward the front door of the house. After contacting an occupant of the residence, the deputy walked back to his vehicle and left. The agent followed the deputy as he drove a block away to the same address on 55th Court. The agent identified himself to the deputy and learned that the deputy was serving some legal papers for the residents at the same address on 55th Court and he had mistakenly approached the residence at 55th Avenue.

What was an honest mistake on the deputy's part led to panic among the residents at the money stash house. After the deputy left their residence, a male came outside while speaking on his cell phone. He was followed by another male and a female. They decided not to return to the residence so they walked to the house of the real estate agent friend of theirs, Maria – the same person who helped members of the organization rent the now abandoned stash houses in Bolingbrook - who lived just a few blocks away.

After they arrived at their friend's residence, we debated what we should do. We did not know where Flaco was as he was not part of the group who had walked away from the Oak Lawn house. He was not at his residence in Tinley Park. Our biggest fear was that the group might decide to relocate their stash house and we would have to find the new one again. But we also felt that finding a new stash house would be much easier now that we had identified several of the organization's customers. Since we were monitoring some of those customers' phones, such as Ponciano and Compadre, we felt they would lead us right back to Flaco who we thought was likely to change the phone we were listening to, just as a precaution. Since we also believed the Oak Lawn house might possibly be vacated because of the deputy's appearance that morning, we decided to take advantage of his mistake and obtain a search warrant for the house. Our thinking was that if we just raided the house in Oak Lawn and left every other suspected stash house alone, it could lead the money group to believe the raid was just an isolated, local law enforcement action and not part of a larger investigation. Our reasoning was sound but the decision to obtain the warrant would turn out to cause far more repercussions than we had anticipated.

AUSA Amar Bhachu and I began working on the affidavit while the rest of the guys kept an eye on the house. We contacted the Oak Lawn Police Department and requested that a squad car be parked in the driveway to prevent anyone from returning and removing anything from the residence.

As we were preparing the affidavit, we started to intercept calls concerning the events of that morning. At 10:00 A.M.,

Choche received a call from the same unknown male in Mexico who had given him the instructions about the cocaine delivery to Saul. The male told Choche he had heard from Felix that "some guys had an 'accident,'" the universal code word meaning someone had trouble with law enforcement. The man asked Choche if he was okay. Choche said he was fine. The man told Choche to "take your precautions," an instruction that meant Choche should change phone numbers and be more conscious of potential police surveillance. Choche then asked, "Is it Flaco or who?" The man replied, "He (referring to Felix) didn't tell me and I didn't ask." About an hour later, Choche called Saul and said, "A guy had an accident. Right now, we are looking into that, to see what happens." Choche told Saul he would call him in two or three days. It was the last call we intercepted over either of Choche's phones. He was obviously heeding his superior's advice and taking his "precautions."

Ponciano and Compadre also received word of Flaco's predicament. At noon, Ponciano called Compadre and told him, "We probably need to find a house because the man from down there just called me and that we shouldn't do anything at all because they got El Flaquito (Flaco)." Compadre expressed surprise and Ponciano said, "Yeah, they got him right now and to change our numbers." Ponciano added, "He told me to be very careful and not go near the office where he would go." Compadre said, "Okay. So now we have to find a new one." It was clear that Ponciano and Compadre had been instructed to change their phone numbers and stay away from the garage at 61st and Homan where Flaco used to take delivery of their drug money. Ponciano and Compadre were going to obtain a new location to make their drug and money exchanges.

Flaco received an incoming call from an unknown male at around one o'clock in the afternoon. Flaco told the male that he would "not be around here these days." Flaco also provided a phone number to the male and told him, "So you could get in touch with a girl here, so you could turn them into her, please."

Flaco was passing a phone number for a woman who, it appeared, would be taking delivery of drug money while Flaco was gone. It was apparent that Flaco was going to leave Chicago for a while, but we did not know where he was at the time of the call. We made no effort to find him because we had no intention of arresting him at this point in the investigation. While we knew he lived in a house in Tinley Park, we were confident that no money or drugs were stored there so we left that residence alone. The money was stored in the Oak Lawn residence. At that time, we assumed Flaco would eventually return to Chicago once he felt the heat from law enforcement had died down.

In addition to requesting a search warrant, we were also planning to request that the search warrant and the underlying affidavit be sealed for a period of thirty days. What we were requesting is called a "delayed notification," which would allow us to execute a search warrant without having to leave a copy of the actual warrant at the residence. The typical service of a search warrant requires us to leave a copy of the warrant, as well as an inventory of the items seized, with the occupants of the residence or, if no one is present, to leave a copy inside the house. Leaving a copy of a federal search warrant at the house would reveal to Flaco's crew that the search was not a local police action and was part of a larger, federal investigation. By obtaining authorization for a delayed notification, we could search the house without having to leave behind a copy of the warrant. A copy of the warrant would have to be provided to the occupants of the house at the end of a 30-day period, unless another authorization was obtained. The reason for our request was to hide both our involvement in the investigation as well as the underlying facts which led us to the stash house in the first place. It's not unusual for members of a drug trafficking group to obtain court documents to determine what law enforcement knows about the organization. Affidavits filed in support of search warrant applications or criminal complaints will contain information that can be useful to an organization in determining the extent of an investigation into their activities. These affidavits can expose the existence of an informant, the use of wiretaps, the extent of surveillance activities, and/or the identification of members of the organization. Trafficking groups can, and do, use this information to alter their drug trafficking activities and take measures to counter our efforts. We are always careful when we file and what we need to disclose in these affidavits. There would be several instances during this investigation when traffickers conducted themselves in a way that seemed to indicate they were aware of some of our investigative tactics.

By obtaining a delayed notification and sealing the underlying affidavit we could prevent anyone from discovering both our involvement in the investigation and what we knew about the organization, for thirty days at least.

While the affidavit for the search warrant presented no probable cause issues for the U.S. Magistrate, he was reluctant to grant our request for a delayed notification. Despite AUSA Bhachu's pleas, the Magistrate was not inclined to give us approval for the delayed notification. The Magistrate's position was that the government could always argue that a delayed notification was necessary, in every case, to preserve the secrecy of an investigation. It was a valid point, which AUSA Bhachu overcame with an argument that we had never intended to execute a search warrant at this point in the investigation but were forced to because of the reaction by the stash house inhabitants to that morning's appearance of a Cook County Sheriff's Deputy at their front door. After AUSA Bhachu made that point, the Magistrate relented and granted us the 30-day delayed notification. While the Magistrate's initial reluctance to grant a delayed notification was frustrating at the time, it would prove to be beneficial to the investigation in the future – exactly 30 days in the future.

With the warrant and the delayed notification signed, the group served the warrant at the house on 55th Avenue in Oak Lawn in the late afternoon. No one was in the residence and there was very little furniture, which is typical of stash houses. In one of the bedrooms, agents found a cardboard box loaded with money that was wrapped in heat-sealed shrink wrap, which is also typical. Whenever cartel employees are packaging money for shipment to Mexico, it is frequently shrink-wrapped in plastic to make it less bulky and less likely to be detected by drug-sniffing dogs. The Food Saver brand vacuum sealer is a favorite choice of most traffickers.

The amount of money in the box turned out to be $2,158,285. We also seized about two and a half kilograms of cocaine, which we hadn't expected to find since this was the money stash house. It's possible that Flaco, like the Accountant in the previous investigation, was authorized to sell cocaine to his own customers outside of La Familia's customers which would explain the presence of those kilograms. We would also recover 22 cell phones, from a residence occupied by no more than three people.

As an added bonus to the seizure of almost three kilograms of cocaine and over 2 million dollars in cash, we recovered several notebooks detailing the collection of money from every cocaine customer in the organization. Every notebook entry was dated and contained the nickname or alias of the customer and the amount of money he had delivered that day. It was an excellent lead that would come in handy in identifying the total number of customers as well as the magnitude of their individual trafficking activities.

As busy as we had been throughout the month of May, by the end of the day on June 2 all five phones that we had been monitoring were turned off. We had made the decision to obtain the search warrant for the Oak Lawn residence because we believed we could get right back onto Flaco and his money crew through the intercepts of Choche, Compadre, and

Ponciano's phones. We had hoped that one or all of those men would keep their phones, but they changed everything. Ponciano and Compadre were also abandoning their "office," the garage at 61st and Homan, as an added precaution. Since no one in the organization knew what had led us to Flaco, they had made the proper assumption that Flaco's phones may have been tapped so they had to change theirs. They also made the correct assumption that Flaco had been followed by law enforcement – he had been, of course – so abandoning the garage at 61st and Homan was a precaution that had to be taken.

Choche turned off his two phones and though he we were sure he remained in the Chicago area, we had no idea where. We had not been able to determine his location before he turned them off. The only clue we had as to Choche's whereabouts had come during the phone conversation between Flaco and Compadre in which Flaco had said Choche was "far away" from Chicago.

Flaco, we would learn later, was driven to a bus station by a relative of Maria. He had jumped on a bus and returned to Mexico that night.

The woman and the two men who had walked away from the Oak Lawn residence in the morning may have returned to Mexico. Their whereabouts were of little concern to us since they were insignificant members of the money group and could be easily replaced by the cartel.

We were starting over.

Chapter 6

We spent the next few weeks completing all the required bureaucratic and legal paperwork for the seizure in Oak Lawn. The seized money was taken to the bank for an official count. With all five phones that we had been monitoring now turned off, we sealed into evidence bags the original computer discs containing the recorded phone calls. The evidence bags were sealed in front of the Chief Judge of the U.S. District Court, which is the mandated procedure under the U.S. code governing wiretaps.

We conducted periodic surveillance of the Oak Lawn residence and Flaco's house in Tinley Park. They were both abandoned. We also discovered that the house on 84th Place, where Choche's runner had loaded the five kilograms of cocaine into Saul's vehicle, had also been abandoned.

We did not have any residences identified for Compadre or Ponciano in Rockford. Even if we did, conducting surveillances of them would not lead us anywhere because they seemed to remain in Rockford while they directed their associate in Chicago to handle drug and money exchanges.

I went through the money ledgers we had recovered from the Oak Lawn residence. They reflected that Flaco and his associates had collected over 17 million dollars from about 30 different cocaine customers between early February and the end of May, 2008, in the Chicago area, an average of about a million dollars a week. As is common with every drug or money ledger, every customer was identified in the ledger by a first name or a nickname only. Most of the customer names were new to us and we had no way of identifying them because we had not recovered a list of phone numbers associated with them.

Of the customers we did know, the ledger showed Ponciano had delivered a total of $487,000 from March to May. The price for one kilogram of cocaine at this time was $18,000. If you take the amount of money that Ponciano delivered and divide it by 18,000, you can assume he received about 27 kilograms of cocaine.

The ledger also contained entries for the customers Squert, Carlos, and Saul, all of whom we had heard making arrangements with Flaco to deliver their drug money.

We spent the month of June trying to find new phone numbers for Ponciano, Compadre, Carlos, Squert, or Choche. We were pretty sure a new money collection group would arrive in Chicago to replace Flaco, if one hadn't already, but the best way to find them was through one of the cocaine customers. Since no enforcement action had been taken with Choche or his drug crew, it was likely that he remained in Chicago.

One phone that did remain in use after our seizure was the one used by the money courier with the van, Ismael. By focusing on him, we hoped he would lead us to the new Flaco. What we learned about Ismael was that he lived in Dallas, Texas, and he ran a legitimate service that delivered packages from Chicago to Mexico. He would drive to Chicago from Dallas in a large cargo van every two weeks and stay at a residence in the 5100 block of South Rockwell in Chicago. He would load the cargo van with packages that people wanted delivered to Mexico. He always left Chicago on a Thursday afternoon at 5:00 P.M. So, every other Thursday, we would watch him collect and load packages all day, but we never saw anything that would lead us to believe he had picked up a load of cash from anyone.

As the end of the 30-day delayed notification period for the search warrant was approaching, I called AUSA Bhachu to ask if we could get another delay from the Magistrate. Bhachu felt it was unlikely that the Magistrate would grant us another delay based upon his reluctance to issue the first one. Bhachu told me to deliver a copy of the warrant and the list of the items we had seized to the Oak Lawn residence before the 30-day period expired.

On June 30, 2008, Special Agent Mike Mokhoff and I drove out to the house. The front curtains were open revealing that the house was still abandoned. I placed a copy of the warrant and the list of seized items by the front door. As we walked back to our cars, we talked about what to do next. Neither of us wanted to return to our office in downtown Chicago and it was too early in the afternoon to start heading home. We decided to go watch Maria's house which was just a few blocks away. It would turn out to be a fortuitous decision.

I parked my vehicle one block north of Maria's residence. Only half an hour later, a red pick-up truck arrived and parked in front of the house. The pick-up truck was the same one we had seen at the Lockwood residence back in April. We had seen it driven by the man who had delivered the eleven kilograms of cocaine we had seized on April 30. A woman exited the driver's side and walked into Maria's house. She was the wife or girlfriend of the cocaine delivery man. She was inside the residence for about twenty minutes before returning to the truck, carrying what appeared to be a stack of mail. She drove away, followed by Mokhoff and me.

Her next stop was the abandoned residence on Lockwood. She walked toward the house and returned to her truck a few minutes later carrying what appeared to be another stack of mail.

After she made a few more stops, we watched her park in the driveway of a residence in the 6500 block of 82nd Place in Burbank. Parked in the driveway was the same beat-up Honda that we had seen parked in front of the Lockwood house back in April. We had found the cocaine delivery man's new home.

It was a fortunate break and it was something that would not have happened if we had obtained another 30-day delayed notification. The only reason we were out on surveillance that day was because we had to deliver a copy of the search warrant. Had we gone back to the office, gone home, or been an hour later arriving at Maria's house, we might never have found the new location. Now we had a place to start, both to find the new cocaine stash houses and the new money crew that we were sure had already arrived in Chicago to take Flaco's place.

Surveillance of the house began immediately. The house was occupied by the cocaine delivery man – let's call him "Brisas" – his wife, and two small children. Within a couple of weeks of the initiation of our surveillance efforts, we had followed Brisas to two other houses in the south suburbs; one on West 84th Street in Justice, and another on West 98th Street in Hickory Hills. Almost every time Brisas would drive to one of those two houses, he would stop about a block away and park on the side of the road. He was making sure he was not being followed. Brisas would remain parked for several minutes. Once he felt comfortable that no one was following him, he would proceed to the house. It was a good sign that those two houses were important to the organization. Both houses also had little outside activity and all the windows were covered up, typical signs of a stash house that we always look for.

We still had not identified any new phone numbers for Choche and we had none for Brisas. We did trash searches for the three residences associated with Brisas, but they didn't provide any evidence of value. Our surveillances of Brisas had not led us to Choche or his residence, nor had they led us to any cocaine customers.

On August 12, 2008, the cocaine customer Saul, who we had intercepted over Choche's phone in May, was arrested in Madison, Wisconsin, by the Dane County Narcotics and Gang Task Force during an unrelated investigation. The day before his arrest, Saul had fronted a half-kilogram of cocaine to an informant working for the police. On the day of his arrest, Saul and an associate were found to be in possession of an additional kilogram of cocaine.

After obtaining the phone records for Saul's cellular phone and running the numbers through one of our agency databases, DEA agents in Madison discovered the link between Saul and our investigation. The agents provided us with Saul's phone records and McConnell identified a phone number that may have been used by Choche. Once again, when McConnell obtained the phone records for that number he learned that it was no longer in use. Choche had dumped it when he learned of Saul's arrest. We still had no idea where Choche was or what phones he was currently using.

We continued our surveillance of Brisas but we still were not seeing anything that looked significant to us. Since we were not listening to any phones and we had no phones numbers identified that looked promising, we decided to approach the residence in Hickory Hills and attempt to gain consent to search the house. We did not have probable cause to obtain a search warrant, but based on our previous experiences with Mexican cartels, we were pretty confident that the occupants of the residence would give us permission to search the house. For whatever reason, the overwhelming majority of individuals who maintain drug or money stash houses will give us consent to search when we ask for it. So, on September 25, 2008, we approached the Hickory Hills residence, rang the doorbell and waited for the residents to come to the door. After a few minutes, two Mexican males came to the door. Neither spoke English and after one of our Spanish-speaking police officers spoke to them for a few minutes, they agreed to let us search the house. There was very little furniture and no one else was inside the residence. We did not find any cocaine or money in the house, but when we went to the garage we discovered two vehicles which contained 108 kilograms of cocaine hidden within them. We arrested both men and took them to the local police station to fingerprint them and check their criminal histories.

With that successful effort under our belt, we decided to approach the residence in Justice. After knocking on the door for several minutes and receiving no answer, two Mexican males came out of the back door of the house and attempted to flee. Both men were quickly apprehended. Again, neither man spoke English and neither had any identification. They also agreed to allow a search of the house. There was little to no furniture and we ended up seizing another 56 kilograms of cocaine from two vehicles parked in the garage. Both men were also taken to the local police department to be fingerprinted.

There were no drug ledgers found in either of the two houses we searched. The ledgers were likely being kept by either Choche or Brisas. The men living in the stash houses were merely watching over the cocaine; they did not make deliveries so there was no need for them to maintain a ledger. And since they were not responsible for making deliveries, they had no list of phone numbers for the customers which was disappointing. Any phone numbers they may have had for Choche or Brisas would not last beyond the end of the day.

All four men arrested that day were determined to be in the U.S. illegally. Fingerprint checks of the men revealed that they had no outstanding warrants and had no arrest records. Because all the cocaine we recovered had been stored in vehicles which were not registered to any of the four men, they could plausibly deny that they were aware the vehicles contained cocaine. Because of that, no charges were filed, and the men were turned over to Immigration and Customs Enforcement ("ICE").

We decided not to approach Brisas' residence for two reasons. One, it was unlikely that any cocaine was stored at his house; he was a courier who made the deliveries but the cocaine was stored at the houses in Hickory Hills and Justice. Second, we intended to continue surveilling him in the hope that he would lead us to Choche.

The cocaine was submitted to our laboratory for chemical and fingerprint analysis. None of the kilograms contained the prints of any of the four men we had arrested. But several prints were lifted from the packages and submitted to the FBI's fingerprint identification system. All the prints were determined to belong to the same man. It was the name of a guy I had come across in another drug investigation ten years earlier. I knew that the man's nickname was "Choche." Up to this point in the investigation, I had assumed the man I knew as Choche back then could be the same Choche we were now looking for, but there was no way to be sure. With the recovery of his fingerprints, there was now no doubt that it was the same guy. I remembered that Choche had been associated with a trafficking group that was transporting thousands of kilograms of cocaine into Chicago. In fact, during that investigation in 1998, we had recovered a drug ledger from the person who was in charge of the drug distribution group at that time. The ledger reflected that the group had brought a staggering amount of almost 12,000 kilograms of cocaine into Chicago in the first five months of 1998. While some portion of that cocaine was likely re-distributed to other Midwestern cities, the fact remains that all of it had transited through Chicago in that short period of time.

Recovering the fingerprints was a great break in the investigation. Not only did we now have Choche positively identified, we had his fingerprints on the cocaine that we could charge him with later. However, we still did not know where he lived, and we had no phone numbers that could lead us to him.

We didn't know it at the time, but after the seizure of the 164 kilograms Choche was replaced as La Familia's head of cocaine distribution in Chicago. Also unknown to us at the time was that members of La Familia in Michoacan were feuding and splitting up. There was quite a bit of fighting amongst various cartels in Mexico during this time. Felix would remain with La Familia and maintain control of La Familia's drug and money crews operating in Chicago, crews that we were now looking for again. Choche would remain in Chicago, but we would not run across him again for many months.

Chapter 7

After the seizures in September of 2008, we continued to conduct periodic surveillances of Brisas' residence, as well as the other organization's cocaine customers or couriers who remained in the Chicago area, such as Manolo and Ismael. We did not observe any significant activity during these surveillances.

Brisas and his wife left their residence in Burbank sometime around the fall of 2008. We now had no locations identified for any of La Familia's drug or money groups in Chicago.

In October, we discovered a residence in the suburb of Bridgeview that appeared to be occupied by individuals who were part of Felix's organization. We conducted several surveillances of this residence. One morning, we watched two men come out of the house and before getting into their car, they got down on their hands and knees and inspected the underside of the vehicle. They were looking for tracking devices. These guys were obviously aware that we sometimes use tracking devices to assist us on moving surveillances. While we had installed tracking devices on several vehicles throughout this investigation, we had not installed one on this vehicle. Once the men were satisfied that their car was tracker-free, they got in and drove away.

Since the men had inspected their car, we knew we could not install a tracker, so we did surveillance without that benefit. We were spotted one day and the house was subsequently abandoned. We never learned who the men were.

In November, we received a cell phone number from agents in our Atlanta office. They believed the number could belong to a new member of the cocaine distribution group in Chicago. We began surveillance to try to find the user of that phone. As we were trying to locate the user of that phone, we learned that another group of DEA agents in Chicago had also received the same telephone number from an informant in an unrelated investigation. It is not unusual for other DEA groups, or other law enforcement agencies for that matter, to come across overlapping targets in drug investigations. We have databases in place to help identify people, locations, or phone numbers that have appeared in other investigations.

The other group's informant had been told that he could call the phone number we were tracking and order 25 kilograms of cocaine. In fact, because the other group had not checked one of our DEA phone databases they did not know that we intended to track the user of the phone and identify his location. Because they were unaware of our investigation, the informant had already contacted the unknown user of the phone and an arrangement had been made for the delivery of the cocaine. Once the other group discovered that the phone number was appearing in our case, it was too late to cancel the planned delivery. We would have preferred more time to locate and identify the user of the phone, but the decision was made to have the informant take delivery.

On November 12, 2008, the informant placed another call to the number. The unknown male who answered told the informant that someone would meet him at a parking lot on Kedzie Avenue, just south of Interstate 55 in Chicago.

At about 4:00 P.M., the informant met with a Mexican male at the parking lot. The male took the informant's car with the intention of returning it once it was loaded with 25 kilograms. The male then drove out of the lot and headed south on I-55. We followed the man to a house in the 300 block of LaCrosse Drive in Bolingbrook, where he pulled into the garage.

About 15 minutes later, the man backed out of the garage and returned to I-55. We were confident that the car was now loaded with cocaine. As the man was driving in the northbound lanes in the direction where the informant was waiting, a marked police car conducted a traffic stop at our request. The man consented to a search of his car and the 25 kilograms were recovered from the vehicle.

With the seizure of the 25 kilograms, we had enough probable cause to obtain a search warrant for the LaCrosse residence in Bolingbrook, where the cocaine had come from. Furthermore, because the information leading to this seizure came from an informant in another independent investigation, we did not need to include in the search warrant affidavit any of the information about our investigation. So, the search warrant was obtained, and it was served that night. There was one person inside the residence, as well as another 46 kilograms of cocaine. It was a nice day, with a total of 71 kilograms of cocaine seized. But, almost as importantly, we recovered a ledger reflecting cocaine distributions to several different customers That ledger was solid evidence that the two men we had arrested this day were part of the new distribution group moving cocaine in the Chicago area for Felix and La Familia. The customer names listed on the ledger included "Squert" and "Carlos" both of whose names we had seen in Flaco's money ledger seized in June in Oak Lawn and had intercepted over Flaco's phone. The ledger also used the same code word for kilograms of cocaine: "machines." The ledger showed that the group had received 150 "machines" on October 9 and another 175 on October 23, 2008. Another entry on a separate page of the ledger indicated that the group may have received another 180 kilograms on November 7.

But the user of the phone number we had been trying to locate, the same number the informant had called to order the 25 kilograms, was nowhere to be found. We had been unable to pinpoint a physical location for the user of that phone and neither of the two men we arrested were in possession of it. The phone, to the surprise of no one, had been turned off after the seizures.

We didn't know it at the time, but the phone we had been looking for was being used by a man called "Panda," and he was the new man in charge of cocaine distribution in Chicago for La Familia. Panda had likely earned his nickname based on his physical resemblance to the actual animal. He had arrived around September and - based on that timing - he was the replacement for Choche who we still did not know was no longer working for La Familia. We would learn later that, after this seizure, Panda left Chicago and went to Wisconsin to live with the customer Squert. Panda would remain in Wisconsin over the Thanksgiving and Christmas holidays before returning to Chicago.

We would also learn much later that Panda had not wanted the delivery of the 25 kilograms to occur. For some reason, he was suspicious of the informant – rightly so - and he had expressed his concerns to Felix sometime after his runner had taken delivery of the informant's car. In fact, during our surveillance of the courier driving the informant's car, we had watched him stop and park in a mall parking lot for a period of time that was long enough for us to suspect that he had spotted our surveillance. Whether he had or not is unknowable, but it was likely that he was waiting for further instructions from Panda who was trying to convince Felix to cancel the delivery. Felix, from the safety of Mexico, dismissed Panda's concerns and ordered him to make the delivery. If Felix had heeded Panda's warnings and called off the delivery, we would not have found the Bolingbrook stash house when we did.

While Panda had dumped the phone that we were looking for, one phone did not get turned off after the seizure. Scattered throughout the pages of the ledger detailing cocaine deliveries were phone numbers written next to a customer's name or nickname. One of those numbers was for a customer named

"Jesse." The ledger reflected that Jesse had received over 50 kilograms of cocaine at the end of October. Even though the ledger we recovered was primarily a drug ledger, it did contain some entries detailing money payments made by some of the customers. The ledger contained entries which indicated Jesse had made payments of $692,000, $500,000, and $450,000, for a total of over 1.6 million dollars, in the first week of November. There was no money recovered, from this drug stash house, and we had no idea where the money might be stored

The phone number associated with Jesse remained active for several weeks after our arrests and seizures. On November 26, 2008, after receiving court authorization to identify the physical location of the phone, we were able to place it inside a residence in the southern suburb of Lemont. Using driver's license information and vehicle registrations of cars that we observed parked at the house, we learned Jesse's full name and date of birth. We now had another cocaine customer identified. He would be another person to follow who could lead us to new members of the cocaine distribution group who were sure to arrive to replace the men we had just arrested. He could also lead us to the money laundering group we knew had to be in Chicago. We had had no success in locating that group since Flaco and his minions had fled Chicago back in June.

As 2008 came to an end, we had seized a total of 259 kilograms of cocaine and 2.1 million dollars from various La Familia workers and customers in the Chicago area. We were about to get much busier in the new year.

Chapter 8

At the beginning of 2009, we again had no known locations for La Familia's drug or money groups. The drug runner Brisas had left Chicago so he was not going to lead us to Choche who we still did not know had already been removed as the supervisor of La Familia's drug group. We had no one identified from the money group who we could follow. The only choice we had was to conduct surveillances of known cocaine customers, but even that option had limits. Ponciano and Compadre remained in Rockford so following them would be a waste of time. The original customer, Manolo, seemed to be no longer affiliated with La Familia so following him was pointless as well. The customer Squert was probably still getting cocaine from La Familia, but we did not know who he was or where he lived, other than in Wisconsin. We did not know the whereabouts of the customer Carlos. The customer Jesse, who we had just identified in November, was the only person who was still receiving cocaine from La Familia and whose residence we knew. So, we conducted several surveillances of him at the end of 2008 and the beginning of 2009, but they did not lead us anywhere significant.

We also followed the money courier, Ismael, every other Thursday when he was in town. Those surveillances were also fruitless.

As frustrating as these surveillances were, we were about to receive a huge break from our counterparts in Atlanta.

In February, DEA agents in Atlanta told us that a few individuals who had been associated with La Familia groups in

Atlanta had moved to Chicago. The Atlanta agents had been investigating La Familia cocaine and money groups operating in their city. Panda, unbeknownst to us at this time, had already returned to Chicago after his Christmas hiatus in Milwaukee with the customer Squert.

The individuals who had been in Atlanta arrived in Chicago sometime in January of 2009. While the Atlanta agents did not know the names or identities of those people, they were able to provide us with the name of a woman who was moving to Chicago with the group. They also gave us information that helped us find an address in Cicero that was associated with the woman. We began conducting surveillance of that location. We were soon able to identify another residence in Berwyn that was associated with the group.

We also began conducting trash pulls at both locations. During one of these trash searches, Stull recovered paperwork for several newly purchased cellular phones. McConnell sent a subpoena to the responsible cell phone company and learned that the phones had been recently activated. The calling records were automatically dumped into one of our databases.

After we discovered these phone numbers, the residences that we had found in Berwyn and Cicero were abandoned. Whether the houses were vacated because someone had spotted our surveillance is not known. But while we had lost track of the physical location of this new group, we now had their new phone numbers and those would prove to be very useful in finding the new locations.

In late February, DEA agents in Alabama learned that a person they were investigating was travelling to Chicago to take delivery of five kilograms of cocaine. Why this person had to travel all the way to Chicago to get a measly five kilograms cannot be explained. It's possible that La Familia had no drug group operating in Atlanta at the time and this customer was forced to drive to Chicago. Whatever the reason, when the agents obtained his cell phone records, they learned that he was calling one of the Chicago numbers that we had just identified from the trash searches at the recently abandoned houses. The agents called McConnell and provided a description of the man and his vehicle as well as a location where he would be staying. It was a house in Cicero. We would find the man and his vehicle at that location.

On February 27, 2009, we were watching the house in Cicero where our Alabama man was staying. In the afternoon, we watched a vehicle drive into the alley behind the house and pull into the garage. After a few minutes, the garage door opened, and the vehicle backed out and left. Half of our surveillance team followed that vehicle, which was driven by one Hispanic male, to a residence in the 1500 block of Cambria Court in Joliet, a suburb southwest of Chicago.

In the meantime, the remainder of the surveillance team continued watching the man from Alabama. We saw him drive away from the Cicero residence and we followed him to the southbound lanes of Interstate 55. We continued to follow him for a short time until we were confident that he was leaving Chicago. At that point, we stopped following him and called the agents in Alabama to let them know their guy was on his way back. We were sure he now had the five kilograms of cocaine in his vehicle and that he had received it from the man we had followed to Cambria Court. The agents would be waiting for him when he arrived back in Alabama.

We now began conducting surveillance of the residence on Cambria Court, which we suspected was a new cocaine stash house. We were also in the process of obtaining various court orders and subpoenas requesting phone records and cellular location authorization. We were still watching the money courier, Ismael, on the Thursdays when he was in town and he was due to arrive in Chicago on Wednesday, March 4. So, on Thursday morning, we set up surveillance of his residence on Rockwell Street in Chicago.

At about 9:30 in the morning, we watched him walk out of the house and get into his large cargo van. We followed him all the way to a Wal-Mart parking lot on Route 59 in Joliet which was about two miles east of the Cambria Court residence. We had never followed him this far away from Chicago and since he was so close to the Cambria house, we were all thinking that he could be picking up money.

He parked in the lot and remained in his vehicle for several minutes. It appeared that he was waiting to meet with someone. A red pick-up truck drove into the lot and the lone male driver contacted Ismael. The pick-up then drove out of the lot followed by Ismael in his cargo van and they both turned west onto Theodore Street. Both vehicles drove a short distance before turning south into a residential neighborhood. But either Ismael or the driver of the pick-up truck saw something they did not like. The vehicles suddenly split up and we lost sight of the pick-up truck. Ismael drove his cargo van back to Theodore and headed west. He pulled into another subdivision, turned around and began heading east back toward the Wal-Mart. He drove slowly and aimlessly on Theodore, and it quickly became clear to us that one or more of our surveillance cars had been spotted. We were unable to find the red pick-up truck anywhere in the surrounding neighborhood.

Ismael left the area and returned to the Interstate. We followed him back to Chicago where he stopped at a Home Depot store on Western Avenue near his house. After he made a purchase inside the Home Depot, we watched him open the rear doors to his cargo van. We could see that there was nothing inside. Ismael had obviously not received any packages from the man in the red pick-up truck.

It was a depressing day for us. We were sure Ismael was about to receive a load of money from the man in the red pick-up truck, but because they had spotted our surveillance the delivery had been called off. We did not know where the red pick-up truck had gone. We kept an eye on the residence on Cambria Court, but the truck never appeared there.

The one positive thing about the day was that we could safely assume Ismael was still working as a money courier for Felix's group in Chicago. With all our prior, fruitless surveillances of Ismael over the past several months, we could never be sure if he still worked for the organization. Now we were confident that he did. We would see him again, sooner than we could know at the time.

We continued to watch the house on Cambria Court in Joliet. On March 12, surveillance agents followed a man from the Cambria Court residence to a house on Brookfield Drive in Joliet. The house was in the same subdivision where we had followed Ismael and the man in the red pick-up truck before we were spotted. Agents conducting surveillance of that Brookfield residence observed a red pick-up truck parked inside the garage.

It would turn out to be Panda's house.

We discovered several phones that we believed Panda and his unknown associates were using. Our pinging efforts helped us identify which phones were being used in which house. It also led to the identification of a third residence in the 16300 block of Fairfield Drive in the neighboring suburb of Plainfield. The pinging showed that the individuals carrying the cell phones we had discovered were moving among the three houses.

We had learned from the Atlanta agents that Panda used multiple phones and changed them frequently. They had also told us that Panda was very cognizant of surveillance, a fact we had learned on our own a few weeks earlier during our surveillance of Ismael.

Because Panda changed his phones so often, McConnell and AUSA Bhachu decided to apply to receive authorization for a "roving" wiretap. While a standard wiretap targets a particular phone, a roving wiretap targets a particular person and any telephone he is believed to be using. With a standard wiretap, if we discovered another phone used by Panda we are required to write another affidavit for that new phone, which can take up to a week or more to receive wiretap authorization. A roving wiretap would allow us to tap any phone we believed was being used by Panda without necessitating another full-blown affidavit. Once a new phone was identified, all we would need to do was send the court order to the cellular company responsible for the phone and file a report with the Chief Judge of the U.S. District Court who had signed the original order. We were still required to file 10-day reports to reassure the Judge that drug-related calls were being made and that Panda was the person making them.

Obtaining a roving wiretap takes more effort than obtaining a standard wiretap. We had to show that Panda used multiple phones and that he changed them frequently. We used information that Atlanta had obtained when Panda was in their city. It was a lot of work, but AUSA Bhachu and McConnell were able to obtain the approval in a matter of a couple of weeks. It would prove to be extremely beneficial to the investigation.

Chapter 9

On April 3, 2009, the Chief Judge for the Northern District of Illinois signed the order that authorized the roving wiretap for any phone used by Panda. Like a standard wiretap, the order was good for thirty days, but now we could listen to any phone that we might discover Panda was using during that time period.

Throughout the course of the wiretap of Panda's phones, we would intercept calls between Panda and Felix in Mexico in which Felix would give instructions to Panda about delivering cocaine or collecting drug money from customers. Unlike the previous year when Flaco oversaw the money group members and Choche oversaw the cocaine group, Panda oversaw both groups, although those groups contained fewer members than the ones that Flaco and Choche had been supervising. Panda would receive instructions from Felix and he would then pass those instructions on to the money group, if the instructions involved money collection, or to the distribution group if the instructions involved a cocaine delivery. We were now in a position to hear everything.

We learned from the calls we were intercepting that there were two men, named "Ruben" and "Choco," who lived at the house on Fairfield. It was clear that they were the ones responsible for picking up money from cocaine customers, counting it, and preparing it for shipment back to Mexico. The house on Fairfield was the money stash house.

The house on Cambria Court was the cocaine stash house. One man, nicknamed "Cheque," was the person responsible for delivering cocaine to customers. Another man, named "Jorge," also lived at the residence with his wife and child. He did not make any cocaine deliveries and his purpose was to provide an outward appearance that a nuclear family lived in the house to cover what was actually occurring.

Throughout the wiretap, Panda would alternate his use of phones, using one to contact Felix in Mexico, another to talk with local customers, and sometimes a third to talk to his crew or the organization's money couriers.

We spent the first two weeks of April trying to identify the customers who were calling Panda to either receive cocaine or deliver drug money from the sale of cocaine that they had received in March, prior to the start of our intercepts. Some of the customers we had heard of before, such as Carlos, Squert and Jesse; some would be new.

On April 4, Panda called Jesse and asked if he had any "papers" to turn in. Jesse said he would call Panda later. About twenty minutes later, an associate of Jesse, named "El Gato" (the cat, in Spanish), called Panda and told him that he would be able to deliver the "receipts" the following day. Later in the day, Panda called El Gato and they agreed to meet the next day at "the Chinese," a coded reference to a location with which they were both familiar, but one that we were unable to determine. After that call, Panda called Ruben and told him to be ready to pick up the money the following day. Panda, using a different phone, called Felix in Mexico and told him that he would be receiving money from Jesse the next day.

While we were unable to surveil the delivery of money from El Gato to Ruben because the coded location was unknown to us, we would intercept calls which revealed that the money had been delivered on the morning of April 5. At 1:33 P.M., Choco called Panda and told him that the money was supposed to be "130," meaning $130,000, but it was "missing three sixty for the one-thirty," which meant that Jesse and El Gato had miscounted their drug money and it was only $129,640 instead of the $130,000 that it was supposed to be.

This was the typical sequence of events. Panda would make arrangements with a customer, in this case Jesse and El Gato, to take delivery of drug money and he would then instruct Ruben or Choco to pick it up. After taking delivery of the cash, Ruben and Choco would return to their house on Fairfield where they would count the money and then report that amount to Panda. Panda would then call Felix and report both the amount of money collected and the customer who had delivered it. Because of those calls, we usually knew how much money was in the stash house at the end of each day.

We also began intercepting new customers. On April 9, Felix called Panda and instructed him to "lend a 'machine'" to a girl named "Anai." Felix told Panda to "lend her one of the old ones to see if she can do something with it." The reference to "one of the old ones" meant a kilogram that was of poorer quality than the other kilograms that were available for delivery. Anai would take delivery of that kilogram on April 11. It was, evidently, a poor quality kilogram because three days later, Felix called Panda and told him Anai would be returning it. Felix said, "Hey, call the young lady, the one who we lent the machine, so you can exchange it for one of the new ones." Panda then called Cheque and told him "to take one 'piece of wood' to the young lady." The phrase "piece of wood" was Panda's code word for kilograms of cocaine; Felix still used the word "machine" which was the preferred code word used by Flaco and Choche the previous year. Panda told Cheque to "bring her one of the new" ones and "pick up the other older" one. Cheque would make the exchange with Anai later that afternoon.

Another new customer, who was nicknamed "Nino," was intercepted on April 12. He would deliver $58,000 in cash the same day we intercepted him. We would later learn that he lived in South Bend, Indiana.

We had not taken any enforcement action during the first two weeks of the wire for two reasons. First, we wanted to conduct surveillance to identify both Panda's drug and money crew members and as many cocaine customers as we could. Second, we could never be sure how Panda would react should we make a seizure of drugs or money. As we had learned throughout this investigation, just being spotted on surveillance was enough to cause people to abandon stash houses or even leave town. We did not want to chase Panda away and be forced to start over again. We would take enforcement action on any opportunity where we felt it was worth the risk.

On April 15, one of those opportunities would present itself.

Chapter 10

At around noon on April 15, Panda called Ruben and told him to start packaging "seven, nine, five, five, zero, zero," which meant that he wanted Ruben to prepare $795,500 in cash for shipment to Mexico. About an hour later, Panda called Felix in Mexico. Panda said that he had received a call from "the mailman" and that he would be delivering money at 4:00 P.M. The word "mailman" was a coded reference to a money courier. Felix told Panda to gather as much money as possible and then asked how much money was on hand. Panda replied that he had $796,853 in cash. Felix then told Panda to "start fixing the seven ninety, please" meaning $790,000. Following that instruction, Panda then called Choco and told him to "start fixing seven nine zero."

At 2:45 P.M., Panda, using a different phone than the one he just used with Felix and Choco, called the courier, who was using a cell phone with a Dallas, Texas, area code. Panda and the courier agreed to meet an hour later. Since the courier was using a cell phone with a Dallas area code, we assumed it could be Ismael. It was a new phone number that we had not come across before. The translators compared the voice of the courier with Ismael's voice from previously intercepted calls and the voices matched. We now knew Ismael was the courier who would be taking delivery of $790,000 from Panda. We would be on the lookout for Ismael's blue cargo van.

After Panda talked to Ismael, he called Felix in Mexico. Felix asked, "Does the guy have an 'office?'" Panda said, "No, he's just passing by." Felix told Panda to "be very careful."

Because Ismael did not have a garage ("office") to take delivery, Felix was concerned that the money would have to be transferred in public view. Felix told Panda to call him after the delivery was made.

Panda called Ruben and told him to drive the money to a laundromat on Laramie Avenue in Cicero. Panda told Ruben to have Choco follow him in another vehicle. Panda said he would meet Ruben and Choco at the laundromat.

We were already watching the residence on Fairfield in Plainfield where Ruben and Choco maintained the drug money. At around 3:15 P.M., the garage door opened and two pick-up trucks backed out. The vehicles, one driven by Ruben and the other by Choco, drove in tandem to Interstate 55. We followed both vehicles north on Interstate 55 to the laundromat in Cicero. After parking their trucks in the lot, Ruben and Choco walked into the laundromat.

At around 4:00 P.M., Panda arrived at the laundromat in his red pick-up truck. At 4:15 P.M., Panda called Ismael and they agreed to meet in five minutes. Ruben and Choco walked out of the laundromat and Ruben got into the driver's seat of one of the pick-up trucks. Before getting into the passenger side of the truck, Choco removed a large black suitcase from the cab and placed it into the bed. They then drove out of the lot and we followed them to a furniture store parking lot on Cicero Avenue. A few minutes later, we saw Ismael and an associate drive into the parking lot in the same cargo van that we had long ago become accustomed to following. After contacting Ismael, Ruben and Choco then led him out of the lot. After several minutes of driving slowly on residential side streets – they were checking to see if they were being followed - they both returned to the laundromat parking lot where Panda was waiting. Ruben then retrieved the large black suitcase from the bed of the truck and placed it into Ismael's cargo van. We knew that suitcase contained $790,000 in drug money. It was amazing to think that Ruben and Choco, two men who were in the

United States illegally and had no driver's licenses or insurance, had driven all the way from Plainfield to Cicero - about 30 miles - with that much drug money sitting on the front seat of the truck. That trip was followed by a short jaunt with the money in the open bed of the truck.

After taking delivery of the money, Ismael drove out of the parking lot. There was no reason to maintain surveillance of Ruben, Choco, or Panda, so we left them at the laundromat and followed Ismael back to the residence on Rockwell in Chicago. When Ismael arrived, we watched him and his assistant carry the suitcase into the residence. We maintained surveillance of the house and the van.

While this surveillance was occurring, Panda called Felix and told him, "All set man. Everything is good," which meant that the money had been safely delivered to the courier.

While we were surveilling Ismael, we intercepted calls from the customer Anai who had drug proceeds to deliver for the kilogram she had received several days earlier. Panda asked Anai, "Were you just going to bring the 'papers?' Or were you going to need 'pieces of wood?'" Anai answered, "That, too." After Panda asked if she wanted "one," Anai replied, "No, supposedly it was going to be ten." Panda said, "Oh, well let me check then."

Panda then called Felix and told him that Anai wanted ten kilograms of cocaine. Felix said, "Lend her nine. Just nine." Panda confirmed, "So I just give her nine." After that call, Panda called Cheque and told him to deliver nine kilograms to Anai. Panda told Cheque that Anai was "around there by the food," a coded reference to the location where Anai was waiting. Panda also told Cheque that Anai was "going to give you the 'receipt' for the wood." Cheque confirmed, "So nine and she is going to give me the receipts." Panda said, "Yeah, the receipts of the other piece of wood that she took." Thirty minutes later at about 6:30 P.M., Cheque called Panda and told him that he had delivered the nine kilograms to Anai and had collected $28,000 from her at the same time. The $28,000 payment was the exact price of the kilogram that Anai had received a few days earlier, which was a significant price increase. The previous year, when Choche and Flaco were in charge, kilogram prices were right around $18,000 each.

We were unable to surveil this delivery or take any enforcement action because we were all watching Ismael. This happens frequently on busy wiretaps. While conducting surveillance of one event, another event is occurring that cannot be surveilled because everyone is occupied by the first event. It would happen again.

Based on our numerous surveillances of Ismael in the past, we knew he would probably be leaving Chicago the next day (Thursday) at around 5:00 P.M. as he always had. But knowing that he now had $790,000 in drug money inside the house, we decided to have a few agents watch the residence throughout the night in the unlikely event that he might change his routine and leave sooner. He didn't.

The next day, April 16, we were all in the area of Ismael's house waiting for him to leave. Throughout the day, people were dropping off packages that they wanted delivered to Mexico.

Around 5 o'clock in the afternoon, Ismael and his assistant began loading packages into the cargo van. They finished loading the van around 7 o'clock. Ismael and his assistant then drove away, eventually entering the southbound lanes of Interstate 57. While we had been unable to observe the black suitcase being loaded into the van, we were sure it was aboard.

We had already made arrangements with our DEA office in Springfield, as well as the Illinois State Police district responsible for that section of the interstate, to conduct a traffic stop of Ismael and his van. While we could have conducted the stop ourselves, we prefer to hide our involvement in these types of investigations. Drug traffickers are aware that we have no marked police cars in our fleet, so a traffic stop conducted by us makes them realize that they are not just the subject of a routine traffic stop. A traffic stop conducted by a marked police car creates less suspicion in the mind of the trafficker that he is the target of a larger investigation. Should a drug or money seizure result from the stop, the trafficker cannot be sure if it was just a lucky break for the police or part of a larger investigation. Using a marked police car is just another way that we try to obscure the extent of our investigation. Even though most traffickers know we use this tactic, it still creates enough confusion that they can't be sure whether they are the targets of a larger case.

As Ismael approached the Springfield area, a state trooper stopped him for speeding. He contacted Ismael and his assistant. After the trooper issued the assistant a written warning for speeding, he asked Ismael for consent to search the van. Ismael agreed. Although we had enough probable cause - based on the intercepted phone calls - to search the van without Ismael's consent, getting his permission to do so causes fewer legal issues later.

Agents and the trooper found the package that we knew Panda, Ruben and Choco had given to Ismael the day before. The package contained exactly $790,000 in cash, neatly wrapped in heat-sealed plastic bags. We weren't surprised to find that money because the calls between Panda, Felix, and Ismael, while somewhat coded, were pretty clear to us. However, what Ismael told us next came as a complete surprise. He told us that he had picked up drug money from two other people besides Panda. He pointed out the other packages inside the van that contained the money. One of the packages contained approximately $400,000. The other package contained approximately 1.5 million dollars. So, a traffic stop that we had expected would net us a seizure of $790,000 in drug money actually resulted in a haul of $2,693,999. It was a surprise to me because I had assumed that Ismael was a dedicated courier for just one trafficking group (Felix/Panda) when he was, in fact, a courier for two other groups who we were completely unaware of. Since most, if not all, couriers working for drug trafficking groups are insulated from the group's operations, Ismael could not tell us anything about Panda or the other two drug groups other than their phone numbers and the locations where he took delivery of their money. The only person in the organization he knew was his brother-in-law, "Beto," who was his sole contact for money pick-ups, a fact we already suspected based on the previous year's wiretap of Flaco's phone.

Ismael knew Panda as "Gordo" and he provided us with the cellular phone number that he used to contact Panda, which was the same number that we had been monitoring. He knew nothing more, other than that he had received the money at the Cicero laundromat which we also already knew since we had watched it happen.

As with Panda, Ismael knew nothing about the other two men who had given him the money to transport other than their phone numbers. We were not surprised to learn that those phones were turned off shortly after our seizure.

After seizing the money from Ismael, we issued him a receipt. Every drug money courier who has money seized by the police wants a receipt to prove to his superiors that he did not steal the money. A receipt from the police usually appeases a courier's superiors, but newspaper articles detailing the seizure are also helpful. The Illinois State Police issued a press release describing the money seizure and a local newspaper printed the story. The receipt and the local news article were sufficient to convince Ismael's superiors that the traffic stop and the seizure was a legitimate police action. It also served to convince his superiors that the seizure was not part of a larger investigation and was just a lucky strike for the police.

Ismael's days as a money courier, however, were over. No organization wanted to take the chance that he was either cooperating with the police or that he was still being watched such that contact with him would attract unwanted police attention. We released him and his assistant that night with the intention of charging them later.

We would later learn at a trial that one of Beto's relatives had been kidnapped after our seizure. He was eventually released after Ismael and Beto convinced the kidnappers that the seizure by law enforcement had occurred and that neither Beto nor Ismael had stolen the money.

The next day, April 17, at around noon, Panda called Felix in Mexico. Felix told Panda, "Cut off communications with the courier because it got messed up." Panda said, "Oh, yeah." Felix replied, "Yeah, throw that cell away." After that call, Panda stopped using the phone that he had used to contact Ismael.

And that was that. Business went on as usual, except that we now had one less phone to monitor.

Chapter 11

After we received an official count of the money from the bank, we needed to obtain court approval to delay making the proper notifications of the seizure. After every drug money seizure, we are obligated to notify any person who can make a claim for the money that has been seized. While notification would be provided to Ismael and his assistant, we were also required to notify Panda because we knew, based on our wiretaps, that some of the seized money had come from him. But sending notification to Panda would obviously alert him to the fact that the traffic stop of Ismael was indeed part of a larger investigation and that it was targeting him. In order for us to prevent the notice from being provided to Panda, we obtained court authorization to delay the notification until the investigation was complete. We would need to obtain this court approval every thirty days.

On April 18, we intercepted a call between Felix and Panda. Felix told Panda that the customer Carlos had "tickets" to be collected. Like "papers," the word "tickets" is frequently used as a coded reference for cash. Felix would provide a cell phone number that Carlos was using. Panda then asked, "Who? Pelavacas or the other one?" Felix answered "Pelavacas." The name "Pelavacas" would turn out to be the nickname of Carlos' backer in Mexico.

Panda called Carlos and said, "They gave me this number to call you on." Carlos asked, "Who is this?" Panda said, "It's me, the kid with wood," a coded reference which meant Panda was La Familia's representative in Chicago for drug deliveries.

Carlos immediately understood and told Panda that he had already spoken to "the people from down there," which meant Mexico. Carlos told Panda that he would call him the following day. Panda then called Felix and told him that he had spoken to Carlos. Panda seemed confused as to what Carlos had wanted until Felix said, "I think that he (Carlos) had some 'tickets' and also might need some 'machines.'"

On April 20, Carlos called Panda and told him he had money to deliver that was "something small." We would watch Carlos turn over money to Ruben and Choco at a fast food chicken restaurant near Cermak Road and California Avenue in Chicago later that day. It turned out to be a very small amount of cash, only $12,000. Later that night, Ruben called Panda and told him they had collected "twelve" from Carlos. Panda's reply was, "That's it? Just the twelve?" Ruben confirmed and then told Panda that he should call Carlos because Carlos wanted to "return some female friends." The phrase "female friends" was a coded reference to kilograms of cocaine that Carlos wanted to return because he could not sell them.

Panda then called Felix and told him that Carlos had delivered $12,000 in drug money. Felix's reply was similar to Panda's. Felix said, "Just twelve pesos?"

On April 24, Panda called Felix and told him that he was going to meet with the customer Squert. Felix acknowledged. About two hours later, Choco called Panda. Panda asked Choco how much money had been collected, using the coded phrase, "What street was it after all?" Choco replied, "One, six, zero…eight, ten," which meant $160,810 had been received from Squert. Panda then called Felix and reported that figure to him. Felix gave approval for Panda to give Squert six more kilograms of cocaine. Felix told Panda, "Make sure you include a variety," which meant that Felix wanted Panda to provide Squert with a mix of both good and poor-quality kilograms. We were not in a position to surveil these activities, but it was clear that Squert had been given six kilograms of cocaine.

On April 25, the customer Nino from South Bend, Indiana, called Panda and told him he would be delivering drug money the following day. Nino would deliver $80,000 to Panda's crew on April 26. He also took delivery of five kilograms of cocaine.

On April 27, the customer Anai had money to deliver as partial payment for the nine kilograms she had received ten days earlier. At 11:00 A.M., Anai called Panda and told him she would be in Panda's neighborhood in forty minutes. Panda said that was fine and then asked, "Are you going to need 'wood?'" Anai said, "No, not right now. I still have some." We decided to surveil this delivery to identify Anai.

At 12:15 P.M., we watched Anai and a male companion arrive at the parking lot of a Mexican restaurant on Route 59 in Shorewood. They arrived in a vehicle with Wisconsin license plates that were registered in the male's name at an address in Green Bay. A few minutes later, Ruben and Choco arrived in a Toyota pick-up truck. Ruben drove by Anai's vehicle and then drove out of the lot. Anai and her friend followed in their car and both vehicles drove in tandem to a Dominick's grocery store further north on Route 59. Both vehicles parked in the lot. Anai got out of her car and walked over to Ruben's truck. We couldn't see her carrying anything, but we knew she was delivering the money to Ruben. After talking to Ruben for a few minutes, Anai returned to her vehicle and left. We followed her and her companion to a restaurant in Chicago. After eating lunch, Anai and her companion left the restaurant. As they were driving away, we asked a Chicago Police officer to conduct a traffic stop of her to get her true identity. The officer made the stop for us and Anai produced a California driver's license. We now had her full name and date of birth. We would later determine that she lived in an apartment building on Jefferson Street in Hammond, Indiana.

While we were following Anai, Choco called Panda and said, "It's been done. We are eating at our office," which meant that the money had been picked up from Anai and taken to the stash house on Fairfield. Panda asked, "Alright then, what street is that house at?" Ruben replied, "By seven, nine." That meant that Anai had just delivered $79,000 in cash.

On May 3, Nino from South Bend, Indiana, delivered $100,000 in cash to Panda's crew.

On May 5, Panda received a call from the customer Jesse. Jesse asked to meet with Panda at a bar on Ashland Avenue and Roscoe Street in Chicago. Jesse told Panda he needed to meet him that day because Jesse was leaving Chicago for a "month and a half." Panda agreed to meet.

Panda then called Felix and told him that he would be meeting with Jesse. Felix told Panda to call him after the meeting and report what Jesse had said.

Around 8:00 P.M., Panda arrived at the bar and met with Jesse and Jesse's associate, el Gato. We not only surveilled this meeting, but McConnell sat at a table next to them and quietly took photos of them with his cell phone.

During the meeting, Panda called Ruben and asked him to retrieve the ledger that maintained a record of the payments made by cocaine customers. Panda asked Ruben to tell him the amounts that Jesse had paid over the past several months. Ruben then proceeded to give Panda those amounts. Jesse had made five money deliveries to Panda's crew between March 22 and April 20 that totaled $520,135. The calls made it clear that Jesse still owed money for previously fronted cocaine and he and Panda were trying to determine the amount that was still outstanding.

After this meeting broke up, Panda called Felix and Felix asked, "What happened with that one? With Jesse?" Panda said, "Well, he said that he would have some 'papers' (i.e., cash) on Saturday but that he is going to head to Cuba...That he is going for about a month and a half, but that if he needs anything he would call me." Felix replied, "No, well what we need is for him to pay." Panda said, "Yeah, the thing is, he said that the guy had 'an accident' around there and that's why he is not going to be here for a while." Jesse was leaving Chicago because one of his associates had had an encounter with law enforcement ("an accident"). He may have been leaving because he felt heat from law enforcement, but it wasn't from us. We were unaware of any enforcement action that had been taken with either him or his associates.

At the end of May 5, Panda and his crew were sitting on a large amount of money that had been collected from several different customers over the past few weeks. It was almost time to send it to Mexico.

Chapter 12

On May 6, 2009, Felix called Panda and told him to start preparing the money he had on hand for another shipment to Mexico. Felix said, "They are going to call you to make a deposit. So, you can start fixing up everything you have." Felix asked Panda to give "me one of your numbers" so that the money courier could call. Panda provided Felix with a phone number, which happened to be one of the phones we were already monitoring. Felix told Panda to call anyone who still owed money and collect as much as possible. Felix told Panda to "fix up nine-forty." That meant Panda and his crew were sitting on at least $940,000 in cash.

That night, Panda called Felix and told him that the money stash house contained, "one, one-hundred, nineteen, three, eighty-three," which meant $1,119,383. Felix told Panda to "fix up about one hundred," which meant exactly one million dollars. A few minutes later, Felix called Panda again and told him, "Listen, put...one-thousand, one-hundred and fifteen. And keep the four pesos there." That meant that Panda was going to prepare $1,115,000 and keep the remaining four thousand dollars at the residence. Felix told Panda to call him when the courier called. After that call, Panda called Ruben and told him to prepare "one thousand, one hundred and fifteen."

We now had a decision to make. We could seize the money after the courier received it from Panda's crew, but would a second large seizure of money cause Panda and Felix to believe their operation was compromised by law enforcement? It was possible. Since the seizure from the courier Ismael on April 16, no money had been sent by Panda to Mexico. Would a second consecutive seizure cause Panda and his crew to leave? It would certainly seem suspicious to Felix and Panda if they lost another large load of money to law enforcement. It was something that we had to take into consideration.

The other option was to watch a delivery to the courier, follow him, and let the money go without seizing it. It was something we considered until the amount of money that Panda was preparing to ship topped one million dollars. At that point, seizing the money became the obvious course of action.

But we were still concerned with what the possible reaction of Panda and Felix might be, so we decided to let the courier get as far south from Chicago as possible. Our thinking was that a traffic stop conducted in a different state – we were considering Missouri or Oklahoma – might be less suspicious to Panda or Felix. Since the seizure from Ismael had occurred in Illinois, we hoped making the seizure in another state might cause less alarm for Felix. The more time and distance we could put between the delivery of money to the courier and our expected seizure of it the better. As it would turn out, it never came to that.

On May 7, we were all conducting surveillance of the Fairfield residence where we knew the money was being stored. We also had one of our surveillance airplanes on stand-by to assist us during the surveillance. Using air surveillance is a great way to prevent drug traffickers from spotting our ground surveillance. Most traffickers are cognizant of our surveillance efforts and they employ a variety of different measures to identify us and our cars, but they almost never know when they are being tracked from the sky. Having the airplane available would come in handy later in the day.

At 8:45 A.M., Panda received a call from the money courier. After making clear to Panda who he was, the courier said that he would pick the money up "more or less after midday." The courier also explained that he knew the location of the cocaine stash house on Cambria Court because he used to deliver "the wood." It appeared that this courier had been a member of the organization's cocaine transportation group. It was the first time we had ever heard from anyone who was a member, or had been a member, of the transportation group. The courier – let's call him "Pedro" - had switched jobs within the organization and was now a money courier instead of a cocaine transporter. I considered it a good career move because Pedro was far less likely to get jail time moving money than he would moving cocaine.

After this call, Panda called Felix and told him that the courier had called, and the money delivery would occur later in the afternoon.

At 2:30 P.M., Panda called Felix and told him that the courier was on his way to take delivery of the cash.

At 3:15 P.M., Panda called Cheque and told him that the courier would be coming to his house. He told Cheque to get into the courier's vehicle and direct him to the money stash house on Fairfield. Because Pedro had been a cocaine courier, he knew the location of the cocaine stash house, but he did not know where the money was stored. Cheque would have to guide him to the Fairfield residence.

At 3:30 P.M., Stull watched as a silver Nissan Frontier pickup truck arrived at the Cambria residence. Cheque came out of the house and got into the passenger side of the vehicle. We then followed the Nissan to the Fairfield residence. We watched the vehicle enter the garage. Special Agent Keith Landa saw Cheque and two other men exit the Nissan and shake hands with Ruben and Choco, who were standing inside the garage. The garage door then closed.

About ten minutes later, the garage door opened, and the Nissan backed out. This time, Cheque was not riding in the vehicle. We knew the Nissan now had over a million dollars inside it.

We followed the Nissan with Pedro and his friend toward the entrance ramps of Interstate 55. As the Nissan approached the ramps, we all expected it to take the southbound lanes and head toward the U.S./Mexico border. It went north instead.

We followed the Nissan to the interchange with Interstate 355, where it continued north. As we were following the truck on I-355, one of our Task Force Officers noticed a Chevy Colorado pick-up truck had been tailing the Nissan. The officer had noticed the Colorado enter the northbound lanes on I-55 in Joliet at the same time as the Nissan. The Colorado was maintaining about a quarter-mile distance behind the Nissan. We were pretty sure that the driver of the Colorado was conducting counter-surveillance, trying to spot any vehicles that might be following the Nissan. This is where our air surveillance came in handy. It allowed us to maintain a comfortable distance behind both vehicles making it more difficult for either driver to spot our surveillance cars.

Both vehicles exited I-355 at North Avenue and headed east. The vehicles traveled in tandem until they reached the city of Elmhurst. Both vehicles then drove slowly through residential and commercial areas, with the Colorado trailing about one block behind the Nissan. They were continuing their counter-surveillance efforts, trying to spot any vehicles that may have followed them from Joliet. We stayed out of the neighborhoods where the vehicles were driving and allowed the air surveillance to watch them. Our air surveillance saw the Nissan drive to an industrial and commercial area on York Road in Elmhurst. The Nissan drove into a non-descript warehouse in the back of a large parking lot. Once inside the warehouse, an overhead door closed behind it. The counter-surveillance man in the Colorado continued driving north on York Road and we let him go.

As soon as our ground units pinpointed the location of the warehouse, our air surveillance departed, and we moved in closer to watch. For the next half hour, we watched as the overhead door sporadically opened and closed. At one point, we could see a flatbed truck parked inside the warehouse. There were at least three men inside. At about 8:45 P.M., the Nissan drove out of the warehouse and headed south on York Road. We decided not to follow it for fear of being spotted. It was obvious that these guys were very conscious of police surveillance. The Nissan returned to the warehouse about an hour and a half later with a large white box in the bed of the vehicle. After the box was dropped off inside the warehouse, the Nissan left again. Again, we did not follow it.

As each hour passed, we knew that we would be maintaining surveillance of the warehouse throughout the night, so we obtained assistance from other agents and police officers who were assigned to other DEA groups. We had no idea how long the money would remain inside the warehouse and since we would not be hearing anything more about it over Panda's phones, we would have to keep a continuous watch. A handful of agents or officers would take our place around midnight while we went home to sleep. We would relieve them first thing in the morning. This rotation process would repeat itself for several days.

We returned early the next morning, Friday, May 8, and relieved the overnight team. Nothing had happened during the night. Later that morning, we watched several men arrive at the warehouse. The men would come and go throughout the day. We maintained surveillance of the warehouse and did not follow any of the men. In the afternoon we watched some of the men return and carry stacks of wood and bags of cement mix into the warehouse. At one point we watched two men arrive and carry what appeared to be bags of fast food into the warehouse. The men left, and the warehouse doors were closed. It seemed to us that someone was staying inside the warehouse overnight. It was a good sign that the money remained inside since it was unlikely that the money would be left alone and unguarded. We speculated that the men were in the process of constructing some type of contraption within which they could conceal the money to ensure the safety of its' transport across the country. A small group of agents relieved us around midnight and they maintained surveillance throughout the night while we went home to sleep again.

The next day, Saturday, May 9, was similar to the previous day. Men came and went, occasionally carrying assorted packages into the warehouse. At one point during the day, Landa could hear what sounded like aerosol spray paint cans being used inside the warehouse.

We were relieved again at midnight, and surveillance was maintained throughout the night into Sunday, May 10. Nothing happened during the night. Sunday was quiet, as no one showed up at the warehouse until 5 o'clock in the afternoon. That person was inside the warehouse for about half an hour before he left.

It's hard to describe the monotony of sitting in your vehicle for 14 to 16 hours every day. We were all getting antsy hoping that something would happen soon.

Our relief crew took over Sunday evening and they continued surveillance throughout the night into Monday morning, May 11.

At 6:40 A.M. on Monday morning, the warehouse door opened, and a man drove the flatbed truck out into the parking lot. The flatbed now had white side-rails installed around the bed. The rails looked freshly painted, which explained the spray paint sounds that Landa had heard on Saturday. A few minutes later, the Chevy Colorado arrived. We could see a man operating a forklift truck inside the warehouse. He placed an object onto the back of the flatbed truck.

At about 7:40 A.M., the flatbed truck and the Colorado left the warehouse together. Our surveillance team chose to remain at the warehouse and not follow the two vehicles. We had become so accustomed to letting men come and go without following them over the past several days that we had grown complacent and assumed the men would return to the warehouse as they always had. It was almost a critical error because this time these guys weren't coming back.

I had been off the radio for a short time – I was inside a Dunkin Donuts – so I had missed hearing some of the activity that was occurring outside the warehouse. When I got back on the radio and heard the vehicles were pulling out onto York Road, I was in a perfect position to fall in behind them. So, I did. Landa had been thinking the same thing as I was because he called me on the private Nextel Direct-Connect phone and asked that I follow both vehicles. There would be no further activity at the warehouse the rest of the day.

I followed both vehicles as they travelled in tandem on York Road. Both vehicles pulled into a Home Depot parking lot in the town of Northbrook. As I drove through the lot, I lost sight of the Colorado pick-up truck, but I saw that the flatbed was parked alone and was now unoccupied. I walked into the Home Depot and found the driver looking at weed trimmers. I knew this guy wasn't looking to buy a weed trimmer. I figured he was just killing time, so I went back outside to look for the missing Colorado.

As I was driving away from the Home Depot, I saw the Colorado returning to the lot. It was now occupied by three men. The Colorado parked next to the flatbed truck and the man who had been inside the Home Depot came out. The four men stood in the lot conversing for a few minutes before the two new arrivals got into the cab of the flatbed and began driving away. The original two men entered the Colorado and they also drove out of the lot. By this time, a few agents from another group had arrived to help me with surveillance. We began following the flatbed truck and let the Colorado go. The Colorado did not return to the warehouse and we would never see those two men again.

What had just occurred in the Home Depot lot was a vehicle drop and driver change. The two new men who were now driving the flatbed truck had been hired to drive the vehicle at least as far as the U.S./Mexico border, perhaps further. The reason the flatbed truck was delivered to the Home Depot lot was because the two men from the warehouse did not want the new drivers to know where the warehouse was. So, the flatbed, which we now suspected was loaded with the money, was delivered to them at the Home Depot. This delivery method kept the drivers unaware of the existence and the location of the warehouse.

We followed the flatbed truck south on Interstate 294 to I-55 where the truck continued south. I felt we could scrap the original plan of making a traffic stop in a state further south and conduct the stop in Illinois. Our original plan was based on the assumption that the money was going to be heading south immediately after being picked up from Panda's crew, so we had wanted to create some time and distance between the delivery and our anticipated seizure. But since the money sat in an Elmhurst warehouse for four days, our time and distance had already been created. We now felt safe in making the seizure in Illinois. Our thinking was that the four-day period between the delivery and the seizure would not cause Panda to be too alarmed by a second loss of money in less than a month. We would turn out to be right.

As we headed south down I-55, I called the supervisor of our Springfield office and asked him to make arrangements with his Illinois State Police contacts for a traffic stop of the flatbed truck. He made the phone call and two squad cars were made available to us.

At about 11:00 A.M., the troopers stopped the truck near Mile Marker 135 on I-55. They contacted the driver and his passenger, who told troopers they were delivering a septic well cover to a city in Illinois whose location they did not know. The troopers noticed that neither of the men were wearing work clothes and there were no tools anywhere on the truck. On the back of the flatbed was an oversize concrete manhole cover.

After a drug-sniffing dog gave a positive alert to the smell of narcotics, the troopers asked the men for consent to search the truck. The men consented, and the troopers asked them to move their vehicle off the expressway to the next exit. They agreed and we all relocated to the parking lot of a seed company in Lincoln, Illinois.

As we searched the truck, we discovered a concrete block, a little larger than a shoebox, in the cabin of the vehicle. It was a strange place for a concrete block and after tapping on it with a metal baton, we realized it was not solid concrete. One of the troopers used a hammer to break the block into pieces. Inside the block was a metal container that contained a large bundle of currency. The amount of money was later determined to be $98,480.

We now turned our attention to the concrete manhole cover sitting on the bed of the truck. One of the troopers tapped the center of the cover with a hammer and it made the same hollow sound as the concrete block had. The trooper began pounding on the cover with a sledge hammer. As the concrete was chipped away, we could see there was a large metal container sealed within. We borrowed a forklift truck from the seed company, lifted the manhole cover from the back of the truck, raised the forks as high as they could go and then dropped the cover to the ground. The force of the cover hitting the pavement was enough to crack the concrete and free the metal container inside. We pried the lid of the container open and discovered eleven plastic-wrapped bundles of cash. The name "Panda" was printed on the outside of ten of the bundles. The amount of money contained within each bundle was also handwritten on the outside of the package. Those amounts totaled $1,115,000 dollars, the exact same amount that Felix had told Panda to prepare for shipment. When it was later counted at the bank, the actual amount would turn out to be $1,114,890, primarily because ninety dollars were determined to be counterfeit.

A Spanish word and the number "250" were printed on the outside of the eleventh bundle. The "250" meant that there should have been $250,000 inside the package and the Spanish word was a reference either to the person who had delivered the money or the person to whom the money was going to be delivered. The money inside that bundle contained $249,590 because 410 dollars were later determined to be counterfeit. Our total haul for the day was $1,462,960.

For the second time in a row, we had seized more drug money than we had expected. Also, for the second time in a row, we learned that there were two other drug trafficking groups (the Spanish name and whoever owned the $98,000 in the separate concrete block) who were using the same money courier as Felix and Panda. This time, however, the two drivers of the flatbed truck had no phone numbers or names of the people whose money was on the truck. Unlike the last money courier, Ismael, these guys had played no role in collecting the cash. They were merely transporting the money long after it had been packaged for shipment. There was almost nothing useful they could tell us, even if they had wanted to.

Both men feigned surprise that money had been discovered inside the concrete block and the manhole cover and they both stated that the money was not theirs. Neither man would tell us where they had received the manhole cover or the truck, which we already knew anyway. We knew we were wasting our time asking questions because neither man could tell us anything more than who had hired them to drive the truck and they weren't telling us that. One of the men then asked the trooper and me for a receipt for the money. Despite his claims that he was unaware he was transporting money, he knew he would need a receipt to show his superiors that the money was seized by the police and he had not stolen it. We wrote one up and gave him a copy.

We brought both men to a local police station and fingerprinted and photographed them. We released them after determining that they had no outstanding arrest warrants. While we had hoped to charge these two men at the end of our investigation, we would not have enough evidence to prove that they knew they were transporting drug money. They had made no admissions to us. As a result, they would never be charged.

During our four-day surveillance of the warehouse in Elmhurst, we had speculated as to the reasons why the money had remained there for so long. The reason, we now knew, was that the men who had concealed the money within the manhole cover had been prepping the flatbed truck and waiting for the cement to dry. The concrete was still a little wet when we broke it open on Monday afternoon.

There was no known reaction to the seizure from either Panda or Felix.

Chapter 13

We spent the day after the money seizure, May 12, working on all our required reports for the seizure. As with the seizure from Ismael, we had to file paperwork to delay the notification of the seizure to Panda. Since we knew Panda's crew had delivered the money, legally they would have to be notified which would obviously alert them to the fact that they were under investigation.

A new customer, nicknamed "Pelon," took delivery of five kilograms of cocaine on May 18. The delivery had been arranged by a man called "Guero," but he was in Michoacan, Mexico, at the time and could not take the delivery himself. So Pelon met Panda and Cheque at a Burger King restaurant on Central Avenue in Cicero. We watched the meeting and were able to identify Pelon. He took the kilograms to an apartment building at Archer Avenue and Seeley Street in Chicago, where he left them in one of the units.

On May 22, a long-ago customer suddenly reappeared. Manolo, the first La Familia customer we had identified in August of 2007 when this investigation began, was back in the picture.

Another group of DEA agents in Chicago had been working an investigation with a law enforcement agency based in Florida. That investigation had developed information that Manolo would be delivering a large amount of drug money to a courier on May 22. Agents from both of our groups set up surveillance of Manolo's residence in Broadview, the same residence we had identified at the start of this investigation. At about 1:15 P.M., we watched as Manolo and his wife came out of the house and placed two duffel bags inside their car. We followed them to a parking lot near the North Riverside mall. A short time later, Manolo and his wife drove out of the lot and began driving toward the anticipated meeting spot for the money delivery. A couple of agents conducted a traffic stop of Manolo's vehicle before he arrived at the location where the courier was waiting. During the stop, Manolo consented to a search of his vehicle. In the trunk of the car was one of the duffel bags which we had seen Manolo place into his car. That bag contained $299,840 in cash. The other duffel bag was found on the back seat of the car and that one contained $399,290 in cash. We also found $2,035 in a man's purse that was located on the back seat. Manolo also had $4,244 in cash in his pants pocket. We seized all the money, which totaled $705,409.

Manolo and his wife were taken into custody and interviewed at the Berwyn Police Department, but they would not provide any information regarding the money that had been seized. It was apparent that Manolo was no longer involved with Felix or Panda and was participating in drug trafficking activity with another organization.

After we fingerprinted Manolo and his wife, and confirmed that they had no outstanding arrest warrants, we released them with the intention of charging Manolo later.

On May 27, Pelon and Guero, who was now in Chicago, delivered $60,000 to Ruben and Choco as partial payment for the five kilograms that Pelon had received on May 18. The following day, Pelon and Guero delivered their final payment of $72,500. The total payment of $132,500 for five kilograms of cocaine meant that Pelon and Guero were being charged $26,500 per kilogram, a reduction in price from what other customers had been paying earlier. It's possible that the price had been lowered because of the poor quality of the cocaine.

On May 27, Squert called Panda and told him that he and his customer, "el Gordo," would be delivering $165,000 the next day. At about 4:00 P.M. on May 28, Squert called Panda and told him he was near Panda's house. Squert told Panda to "send that guy" (referring to either Ruben or Choco) to pick up the "receipts" from el Gordo. Squert said he would go to Panda's house while Ruben took delivery of the cash from el Gordo at another location.

Stull happened to be near Panda's house at the time and he saw a Ford Ranger pick-up truck with Wisconsin license plates parked in the driveway. The plates were registered in Squert's real name at a residence in Brookfield, Wisconsin. We now knew Squert's identity. We did not know, however, where Ruben and Choco were meeting "el Gordo" so Stull was not able to identify him or his vehicle. Later that night, Panda confirmed with Felix that Squert had delivered $165,000 in cash.

Chapter 14

At the beginning of June, we discovered that some of Panda's crew had completed their tours of duty in Chicago and they intended to return to Mexico within a week. This forced us to end the wiretaps of Panda's phones and make arrests. Because this development had caught us off guard, we had only enough time to get warrants for Panda and his drug and money crews. We did not have enough time to prepare warrants for all the customers who we could charge so we would have to conduct a round-up of them later. It was a disappointing development but there was little we could do about it. We would have preferred to continue the wires to identify more customers but that was not an option that we had.

We decided to get arrest warrants just for Panda, Ruben, Jorge, Cheque and Choco, as well as search warrants for the three houses they lived in. All the customers would be charged and arrested later. Because we intended to charge the customers later, we did not want to expose the extent of our investigation at this time. A criminal complaint would reveal to Panda and the boys the wiretaps we had conducted, which could tip off the customers that they were on our radar and they would be next. We could delay the exposure of the extent of our investigation by obtaining indictments.

Obtaining an indictment, as opposed to filing a criminal complaint, would prevent the immediate disclosure of the facts and the evidence we had gathered against the group. Had we filed a criminal complaint, it would have required a detailed recitation of the evidence against Panda, Ruben, Jorge, Cheque and Choco which would have exposed the extent of the wiretaps and surveillances we had conducted. That evidence needs to be spelled out in an affidavit for a federal judge or magistrate to make a proper determination as to whether probable cause exists to charge the men with drug trafficking offenses. A copy of the complaint is given to the defendants at their initial appearance before a magistrate which is required, in Chicago, to occur within seventeen hours of an arrest.

With an indictment, the evidence is submitted, in secret, to a grand jury who then make their determination as to whether there is probable cause to support the drug trafficking charges. Once the grand jury decides to indict, only the charges are revealed to the defendants at their initial appearance. The supporting facts and evidence are not revealed to the defendants until a later date. By charging the defendants via an indictment rather than a criminal complaint, we could delay the exposure of our investigation thereby giving us additional time to prepare the charges against the customers.

While we were scrambling to prepare the indictments and search warrants, the customers Ponciano and Compadre reappeared. We had lost track of them since we were so busy with Panda's phones. Now, on June 9, just a few days before Panda was scheduled to be arrested, Felix called and told Panda to "lend three machines" to "Ponciano." Fifteen minutes later, Panda called Compadre and arranged for the three kilograms to be delivered.

At 2:30 in the afternoon, we followed Cheque from the Cambria residence and watched him arrive in the 1400 block of South 58th Avenue in Cicero. He drove into an alley and pulled into a garage, but we could not adequately determine which garage he was in. We had no plan at that time to seize the cocaine but even if we had, we did not know which garage it had gone into. We did not see Ponciano or Compadre in the area, so it was possible that they had remained in Rockford as they usually had during the wiretap of Flaco in 2008. Once we saw Cheque driving out of the neighborhood, we terminated surveillance.

About two hours later, a man named Javier, an associate of Ponciano and Compadre, called Panda and asked, "How long do you think it will take your guy to stop by the office for the 'papers?'" Panda said that it would take about an hour. In coded language, Javier said he had money for one of the kilograms and would have the cash for the other two the following day.

Landa happened to be nearby the 58th Avenue address in Cicero. At 5:30 P.M., he watched as Ruben, Cheque, and Choco arrived in a tan Toyota pick-up truck. All three men entered a residence which Landa was now able to identify. A short time later, all three came out of the house, got into the Toyota and left. Cheque later called Panda and told him they had picked up $26,000. In another apparent concession to the poor quality of the cocaine, the kilogram price had been reduced from the original $28,000.

The following morning, June 10, Felix called Panda and told him to call "Ponciano" because they had more "tickets" to deliver. Panda then called Compadre and made the arrangements. Ruben and Choco would take delivery of $52,000 from Javier at the house on 58th Avenue. Agents watched Ruben drive his vehicle into the garage behind the residence that Landa had identified the day before. Ruben was inside the garage for a short time before leaving.

At 2:00 that afternoon, Compadre called Panda and said, "Let's see if you can do 'two hours,'" which was a coded reference meaning two kilograms of cocaine. Panda replied, "Two hours?" Compadre said, "yes." Panda then called Cheque and told him to "take two to the man which you took to them yesterday."

Since we now had the garage identified and we knew that Panda was soon to be arrested, we decided to try to intercept the two kilograms after Cheque dropped them off.

At 3:00 P.M., we watched Cheque leave his residence and drive to Cicero, where we saw him pull into the garage behind the residence. After a few minutes, Cheque backed his vehicle out of the garage and drove away. We let him go and continued to watch the garage.

At 3:40 P.M., a green Ford mini-van drove down the alley and pulled into the garage. The garage door closed and then re-opened about fifteen minutes later. The mini-van backed out of the garage and drove out of the alley. We followed it, knowing that it probably contained the two kilograms of cocaine that Cheque had just delivered.

We followed the van to the westbound lanes of I-290 and at 4:30 P.M., we had a Cook County Sheriff's Officer conduct a traffic stop for us. The driver was Javier and he had no driver's license or insurance. Javier was taken into custody and brought to the Arlington Heights Police Department for processing.

Based on our observations on surveillance and the intercepted phone calls, we had probable cause to search the mini-van. We searched the van at the police department and we found two kilograms of cocaine in a factory-installed compartment in the rear cargo area of the vehicle.

We fingerprinted and photographed Javier. We tried to interview him, but he had nothing to say so we released him. We would be charging him later with the rest of the customers.

Panda learned of the seizure the next day. On June 11, at noon, Felix called and told Panda, "Be careful over there. Change the phone that you used to talk to Ponciano on because he called me a little while ago, and they had an 'accident' yesterday." Panda said, "Oh, Ponciano's guy?" Felix said, "Yeah, that guy."

So, Panda dumped that phone but it no longer mattered. We had our indictments and our search warrants, and we would be executing them the following day. We had a pretty good idea what we could expect to find.

Chapter 15

On the morning of June 12, 2009, everyone involved in executing the arrest and search warrants met at a WalMart parking lot in Bolingbrook. Our plan was to ensure that each arrest team hit their assigned residence at the same time to prevent any one of our defendants from warning the others. With the teams assembled, everyone headed to their assigned residence. At 6:40 A.M., with every team in place, all three residences were approached by the search and arrest teams.

I was assigned to Ruben and Choco's house on Fairfield. As we pulled up in front of the house, I noticed the neighbors on the other side of the street were outside setting up a yard sale. It struck me that they had front row seats to watch our impending raid. We knocked on the front door and after not receiving a quick-enough response from the inhabitants, we breached the door and made entry into the house. The first two agents raced up the stairs and found Choco in one of the bedrooms. I was third through the door and I turned toward the living room to the left, where Ruben and his wife had been sleeping on the floor. Neither Ruben nor Choco resisted and they were placed in handcuffs. We searched the rest of the house for any other individuals. Besides Ruben's wife, there was an infant child and a young boy. It was unknown to us before we served the warrants, but Ruben's wife was Jorge's daughter.

The house was sparsely furnished, like most stash houses, and as we searched we could not find the money that we suspected was there. At one point, Stull came up to me and with a nervous laugh asked, "It's gotta be here, right?" I laughed and said that it should be.

Someone then noticed an attic access panel in the upstairs hallway. We found a ladder and Stull climbed up to look. He saw several heat-sealed bundles of cash partially hidden among insulation foam. After taking pictures of the bags, he began lowering the bundles to me. The total amount of money that was in the attic was later determined to be $1,365,414, which was what we had expected to find.

Once we found the money, we conducted a more thorough search of the residence. In addition to finding a heat sealer and boxes of rubber bands – the typical tools of a group responsible for counting and packaging drug money - we also found eighteen cellular phones and a money ledger recording all the payments that had been made by the various customers. The entries in the ledger would match up nicely with the phone calls that we had been intercepting about money deliveries.

Meanwhile, McConnell's team had executed the warrant at Panda's house. Like Ruben and Choco, Panda also did not come to the front door, so it had to be breached to gain entry. They found Panda hiding in one of the bathrooms. No one else was present inside the residence.

As we had suspected, Panda had no drugs or money stored at his house. Panda had not been maintaining the drug or money ledgers. He was cooperative, but he made no statements.

After making entry at the Cambria Court residence, agents arrested Jorge who offered no resistance. Cheque was found hiding in his bedroom closet but he also offered no resistance once he was discovered. Jorge's wife and child were the only other people in the house.

During the search of the house, agents found 20 kilograms of cocaine on the floor of a closet in an upstairs bedroom. Another 34 kilograms of cocaine were found within a hidden compartment of a Ford F-150 pick-up truck that was parked in the garage, for a total of 54 kilograms.

After all the searches were completed, the five arrestees were transported to an Immigration and Customs Enforcement ("ICE") facility for processing. Jorge, Cheque and Panda all had previous immigration issues or outstanding warrants, so ICE was able to file charges and detain them.

Ruben and Choco were different. Neither had arrest records and neither had previous immigration violations. For legal reasons, we reluctantly released them both at the end of the day.

While it would take several weeks for our laboratory to test the kilograms we had seized, when the results came in we were surprised at how poor the quality of some of the cocaine really was. The twenty kilograms we had seized from the closet tested out at a purity level of 51%, which is awful. Good quality kilograms at the wholesale level should have a purity in the 90 percent range. It was no wonder that some customers had been requesting exchanges or returns and the price had been reduced.

With Panda, Jorge and Cheque safely housed in ICE facilities, we began preparing the affidavits for the next round of arrests of the organization's customers.

Chapter 16

To prepare the criminal complaint, McConnell, Stull and I met with AUSAs Bhachu, Donovan and Baker to discuss the evidence we had against every person we came across during the wiretap investigation. The bulk of the evidence would come from the calls we intercepted and the seizures we had made. The cocaine and money ledgers that we had just seized from the Cambria and Fairfield stash houses would also help us prove the total number of kilograms that had been distributed to each customer, as well as the amount of drug money that had been collected. The numbers recorded in both ledgers matched the numbers we had intercepted over Panda's phones.

The first person we intended to charge was Manolo, the customer we had identified at the beginning of the investigation. He had been intercepted over Atlanta's wiretap in August of 2007, we had his name in the first Bolingbrook drug ledgers detailing the amount of cocaine he had received, and we had seized a large amount of drug money from him in May of 2009.

In addition to determining the evidence we had against each person, we also had to prove how we knew that person was the same one intercepted in the phone calls, which is made more difficult by the fact that few phones are subscribed in the true name of the user. In most cases, we can make a positive identification through surveillance. For example, if we intercept a call in which a participant says he will be in a specific location at a certain time, surveillance can observe who shows up at that spot and record the license plates of the vehicle. In Manolo's case, we had intercepted him in July of 2007 saying that he was driving a black Jeep and was in the Cermak and Harlem Avenues area. Surveillance agents saw him driving a black Jeep in that exact spot. The Jeep's license plates were registered in his name. We obtained his driver's license photo and we determined that the picture matched that of the person we had seen driving the Jeep.

Since we know that we will need to prove the identities of the people we intercept during wiretaps, we make every effort throughout the investigation to make those positive identifications.

We wanted to charge the three men we had arrested during the seizure of 11 kilograms of cocaine in April of 2008, but the AUSAs felt that we did not have enough evidence to convict. Since the kilograms had been recovered from a hidden compartment in the men's truck, each man could plausibly deny that he knew the kilograms were in the truck. We also had not been intercepting any phone calls during that time, so we did not have any of these men on tape discussing the delivery. As a result, no charges would be filed against either of the three men.

We had enough evidence to charge Celso ("Ponciano") and Compadre, the two brothers from Rockford, as well as their drug runner, Javier. The traffic stop we had conducted of Javier on June 10 served as the confirmation that he was the same Javier we had heard on Panda's phone. We had fingerprinted and photographed him following the stop and the seizure of the two kilograms of cocaine.

Celso and Compadre's identities had been determined during separate traffic stops, on different days, conducted by the local police at our request. In addition to providing identification, both Celso and Compadre made phone calls after their respective stops complaining that they had been stopped. In Celso's phone call, he referred to the police who stopped him as "fucking dogs," "sons of bitches" and "assholes." The phone calls confirmed we had correctly identified the right people. It also seemed, to me at least, that both Celso and Compadre were aware that we used that tactic to identify people. Compadre had expressed concern that his stop was not for the traffic offense he had committed but for something else. He was right to be concerned, of course, because the stop was about more than just the traffic violation, but the fact that he was suspicious led me to believe he suspected something more serious.

Squert was next and confirming his identity was simple. The cell phone he used to speak with Panda was registered in his real name, which almost never happens with drug traffickers. In addition, Stull had seen Squert at Panda's house on May 28 at the same time that Squert had said he would be there. Stull recorded the license plate number of Squert's vehicle and it was also registered in his real name. We also conducted surveillance of his home in Brookfield, Wisconsin, and confirmed that he lived there.

The identities of the courier Ismael and his associate, whose name was Oscar, had been determined at the time of their traffic stop and the seizure of 2.6 million dollars on April 16, 2009.

The customer Carlos had been identified during a surveillance when he met with Flaco in May of 2008 and again when he met with Ruben and Choco to deliver $12,000 at the chicken restaurant at California and Cermak in Chicago in April of 2009.

The customer Anai had been identified on April 27 during a traffic stop conducted after she delivered money to Ruben. We tracked her to an apartment building in the 6600 block of Jefferson in Hammond, Indiana. We would subsequently observe the vehicle that we always saw her in – the one with the Wisconsin license plates - parked in a small lot behind the building.

We were also able to charge the customer Nino who resided in South Bend, Indiana, whose identity had also been positively determined during the wiretap of Panda's phones.

We had identified the customer Jesse in November of 2008 and our confirmation that he was the same Jesse intercepted on Panda's phone came when he had called and arranged to meet Panda at a bar on the north side of Chicago on May 5, 2009. Surveillance agents had watched him meet Panda at that bar. That same surveillance also confirmed the identity of Jesse's associate, El Gato, who was at the same meeting. McConnell had taken good pictures of them while he was seated at a table next to them.

The customer Pelon had been identified on May 18 when he met with Panda at the Burger King on Central Avenue in Chicago.

Panda, Cheque, and Jorge had obviously been identified when we arrested them on June 12. We had done voice identifications during their processing at the ICE facilities. Our contract translators confirmed that the voices of the men we had in custody matched the voices of the men we had been intercepting over Panda's phones.

We also charged Saul, the customer from Wisconsin who we had intercepted over Choche's phone in May of 2008. He had remained in custody following his arrest in Madison in August of 2008.

While we were compiling evidence and proving the identity of the people we had intercepted during the wires, we were also ensuring that we had the current addresses of each person we intended to arrest. We were preparing "arrest packages" for each defendant and it was imperative that each package had the current residence for the arrestee. We conducted numerous surveillances of each defendant to confirm we had their correct addresses.

One person who we could not find was Choche, the cocaine distribution group supervisor in 2008, prior to Panda. We had plenty of evidence to charge him; his fingerprints were on the cocaine we had recovered from the stash house in Hickory Hills in September of 2008. Choche also had an outstanding arrest warrant for immigration violations, so if we could find him we could arrest him and have ICE hold him until our drug charges were filed. But we had had no contact with him since the Hickory Hills seizure. That was about to change.

In July of 2009, another group of DEA agents in Chicago were investigating a group of money launderers and couriers. During one of their surveillances, they followed a man to a residence in Chicago that we knew had been associated with Choche. We met with the agents and they told us that they were expecting a delivery of money to a courier to occur on July 14, 2009, in the Kankakee, Illinois, area. Based on the information that they had developed, we believed Choche could be one of the guys delivering the money.

At the same time this other investigation was occurring, we were in the midst of reviewing all the surveillance reports we had written throughout our case. During our surveillances of Brisas, the cocaine courier for Choche, and the Hickory Hills and Justice stash houses in 2008, we discovered a vehicle had been observed that was registered to an address in Kankakee. At the time, we did not know the significance of the vehicle. We had never checked out the address because we had assumed it was another non-existent location. Up to that point in the investigation, we had come across so many vehicles that were registered in false names or registered to addresses that did not exist that we had grown accustomed to conducting only perfunctory checks of the registered owners and addresses of those vehicles. With Choche now popping up in another investigation which was expecting a money delivery to occur in Kankakee, perhaps that Kankakee address we had overlooked in 2008 really did exist. And perhaps Kankakee was what Flaco had meant when he told Compadre in May of 2008 that Choche was "far away" from Chicago. Kankakee is about 60 miles from downtown Chicago.

I drove out to the address in Kankakee and found that it did exist, but it was abandoned. It was a small house surrounded by a large parcel of farmland. There were no vehicles in the driveway, the windows had no curtains and one of the glass panes was broken. Maybe Choche had lived there at one point but he surely was not there now.

On July 14, 2009, agents from both of our groups established surveillance in the Kankakee area. I provided a picture of Choche to a Kankakee Police officer who was going to conduct the traffic stop of the vehicle that was expected to be delivering the cash. The money was supposed to be delivered to a courier who was waiting at a shopping mall in Matteson. We did not know exactly where the vehicle would be coming from, but we did know it was coming out of Kankakee. So, we were all positioned in different locations along Interstate 57 watching the northbound lanes trying to spot the vehicle.

At about 3:00 P.M., someone saw the vehicle driving north on the interstate and called it out on the radio. The Kankakee officer caught up to the vehicle and conducted the traffic stop. There were two occupants and they both consented to a search of their car. The officer found a suitcase filled with cash in the trunk. Both men were taken into custody and transported to the Kankakee Police Department. The cash in the suitcase was later determined to be $570,061.

The officer reported to one of the agents in the other group that neither of the men in the car matched the photo that I had given him. When that information was passed to McConnell and me, we left. Since Choche was not present, this was not our case so there was no reason for us to stay. The other group of agents was in charge of conducting the investigation.

The next day, one of the agents from the other group gave McConnell and me the identities of the two people who had been stopped and arrested. I immediately recognized one of the names as one of Choche's aliases. Choche had, in fact, been one of the two people in the car delivering the money the previous day. The photo I had given the officer was a ten-year old arrest photo – since we had not seen him on any of our surveillances we had no recent photo of him - and the officer had not recognized either of the occupants as Choche. So, we had Choche in custody but he had already been released by the time we learned of it. He had also given the arresting officers an address where he did not live, which was disappointing but not surprising. We still had no place to look for him, but now we at least knew that he lived somewhere in the greater Kankakee area.

But finding his residence turned out to be much easier than I had anticipated. The house in Chicago that we had associated with him was registered in one of his relative's names. Choche was in the U.S. illegally and he had no property in his name. So, I ran his relative's name through a public real estate database. The database revealed that the relative had recently taken possession of a property in Danforth, a city just south of Kankakee.

Similar to the abandoned house in Kankakee, the Danforth property contained a small house surrounded by a large area of farmland. There was also a large barn and an outbuilding on the property. We conducted numerous surveillances and while we saw several individuals milling about the property, we could not positively identify Choche as one of them. What made surveillance of that property more difficult was the lack of a good vantage point from which to watch. The only viable option from which to observe the farm was to sit in a cornfield located directly across the street. I was surprised to discover there is quite a bit of room for a person to maneuver between the rows of six-foot tall corn stalks. Although we didn't see Choche at the farm, the vehicles that were parked in the driveway were registered to names and addresses that we had previously associated with him. We were confident that he was living at this location.

At the same time we were conducting these surveillances and preparing the complaint, the Mexican federal police arrested Arnoldo Rueda-Medina, one of La Familia's top leaders in Michoacan. The arrest occurred on July 11 and was immediately followed by armed attacks on police stations throughout Michoacan, as well as the states of Guerrero and Guanajuato. One of the attacks was launched on the police facility where Rueda-Medina was being held in an attempt to free him. The attempt was unsuccessful, and Rueda-Medina was quickly hustled out of Michoacan to a prison in Mexico City. The violence continued for at least four days after Rueda-Medina's arrest. The attacks resulted in the deaths of five police officers and two Mexican soldiers, as well as the wounding of at least ten other officers. In addition, twelve off-duty Mexican federal agents were ambushed and abducted in Michoacan. Their bodies were found on July 15 dumped alongside a road near the town of La Huacana, Michoacan. They were found stacked in a pile - semi naked except for the one female among them - with their hands tied. All twelve had been shot in the head and their bodies showed signs of torture. A note had been left with the bodies that read, "So that you come for another, we will be waiting for you here," an obvious threat to the Mexican police that any further arrests of other top La Familia leaders would be met with additional violence. It was not an idle threat. It was also a reminder of the extreme violence that La Familia was capable of, at least in Mexico. In Chicago by contrast, with all the searches, arrests and traffic stops we had conducted to date, we had not recovered a single weapon from any La Familia worker or customer.

In mid-August the affidavit for our criminal complaint was complete. It was 177 pages long. We had good locations for everyone we intended to arrest. Agents and officers had been assigned to arrest teams for each defendant. The arrests would all take place on the morning of August 25, 2009, with one exception. We were going to try to find Choche at the Danforth location on August 24 and arrest him using the outstanding ICE warrant. ICE had already agreed to hold him until our drug charges were filed.

Chapter 17

On Monday morning, August 24, Stull, Landa, and I met three ICE agents at the Illinois State Police post in Ashkum. We all put on our bullet-resistant vests and headed to what we hoped would be Choche's house.

We all pulled into the driveway and contacted a woman who was near the house. She allowed one of the ICE agents and me into the house. He and I searched the residence but Choche was not inside. Stull, Landa and the other ICE agents fanned out across the property. As they approached the barn, Choche came walking out. He offered no resistance and was placed in handcuffs.

I could now see why the Kankakee officer had not recognized him in July when he had Choche in custody; he looked nothing like the arrest photo I had provided the officer. Even now, I wasn't sure we had the right guy although Stull had no doubts. The ICE agents had a mobile fingerprint machine and they took Choche's prints. The prints matched; the guy we now had in custody was the same guy we knew to be Choche and the same guy whose fingerprints were on the kilograms seized in Hickory Hills.

Choche did not speak English so one of the ICE agents asked him in Spanish if we could search the property. Choche said no. I called AUSA Bhachu and let him know that we had Choche in custody but that he would not consent to a search of the property. Bhachu and I discussed obtaining a search warrant but we both agreed we had no probable cause to get one. In any event, it was not likely that there was any cocaine stored on the property; Choche was not the guy to make that kind of mistake. While he had made the mistake of leaving his fingerprints on the kilograms at the stash house, he would never allow cocaine to be stored at his personal residence. It was possible that he had drug money hidden somewhere on the property, but if he did we would never know.

After we identified all the people who were present on the property, we left. ICE took Choche to their detention facility. We would take custody of him sometime after our charges were filed which was scheduled to occur the following day.

On the afternoon of August 24, I signed the affidavit for the criminal complaint before U.S. Magistrate Judge Maria Valdez. We now had our arrest warrants for everyone listed in the complaint. We held a briefing for every agent and Task Force Officer who would be participating in the next day's events. At this briefing, every individual team is provided with an "arrest package" detailing their specific assignment. Each package contains the identifying information and a photo of the person to be arrested, a print-out of their criminal history if they have one, the address where they most likely will be found and any other relevant information regarding the arrestee. A copy of the arrest warrant is also contained within each package, as well as a copy of a search warrant if one was obtained. With the briefings complete, everything was ready to go for the next morning.

At 6:00 A.M. on August 25, every team approached their assigned residences. I was the team leader of the group assigned to arrest Anai in Hammond, Indiana. My original six-man team consisted of a combination of DEA agents and Deputy U.S. Marshals. Since we have a DEA office in Indiana that is responsible for Hammond, I had called the supervisor and asked if he could provide a couple of agents to assist us. To me, "a couple" means two. To him, "a couple" apparently meant everybody. He ended up bringing out his entire group of agents and police officers. We wound up with almost 20 agents and officers to arrest a short, soft-spoken, twenty-two year old Mexican-American woman. It was a little embarrassing. To see us that morning, you would have thought we were going after an entire biker gang.

We found Anai in her apartment in Hammond and, despite the size of our force, quietly took her into custody. She was transported to our Chicago office for processing and an eventual appearance before U.S. Magistrate Valdez.

Most of the other arrest teams were successful in locating their defendants. Celso, Carlos, Jesse, El Gato, Pelon and Squert were all arrested at their residences. No one offered any resistance. The money courier Ismael, as well as his associate Oscar, were allowed to turn themselves in at a later date. Manolo would be arrested a few days later. Panda, Cheque, and Jorge were already in custody. The current complaint would supplant the one we had filed at the time of their arrests in June. The customer Saul was also already in custody in Wisconsin and he would be transferred to our judicial district to face our charges later.

We could not find Compadre or his associate, Javier. We learned later that Compadre had been in Mexico when we conducted our round-up. We also could not find Nino at his house in South Bend. Nino would pop up in an investigation conducted by our DEA office responsible for South Bend many months later. He would be prosecuted in the Northern District of Indiana and our charges would be rolled into their case.

In addition to the arrest warrants, we had obtained search warrants for some of the arrestee's residences: Celso's house in Rockford, Manolo's house in Broadview, El Gato's in Chicago, Jesse's in Orland Park and Squert's in Brookfield, Wisconsin. Nothing of significance was seized from any of the houses. Agents seized about $9,000 in cash from Squert's residence, but that was it. Some of the other arrestees consented to searches of their residences but nothing significant was seized from those either.

We did, however, arrest one other person who had not been charged in our initial complaint. After completing his assigned arrest duties, McConnell went to the residence of a person we believed was a cocaine customer of Carlos. His name was Edwin and we had intercepted him talking to Panda so we had his voice on tape. McConnell knocked on the door of Edwin's residence and he answered. McConnell played the tape-recorded phone call for him and he confessed that he had been receiving cocaine from Carlos. McConnell called AUSA Bhachu and after explaining what had just occurred, Bhachu agreed to file charges against Edwin. McConnell took him into custody and an amended affidavit was filed to add Edwin to the complaint.

All the arrestees were transported to our Chicago office where they were fingerprinted and photographed. We attempted to conduct interviews but every one of the arrestees refused to answer questions and requested their lawyers. That was fine with me. No interviews meant we would spend less time writing reports documenting what was said. We had plenty of evidence, so we did not need anyone to confess. As it turned out, everyone we arrested this day would waive their rights to a jury trial and plead guilty. But we still had a lot of work to do before that happened.

Every defendant was scheduled to be brought before Magistrate Valdez for their initial appearance, a court proceeding where they and their attorneys receive a copy of the complaint containing the charges filed against them. It would be the first time that the extent of our investigation would be revealed. Choche had been removed from the ICE detention facility by one of our Task Force Officers, Danny Gutierrez, to appear at this hearing. As TFO Gutierrez was driving his vehicle, with Choche inside, down a ramp which led to the basement of our building, a security barrier began to rise as he drove over it. The barrier punctured his vehicle's gas tank. Nobody was hurt but the vehicle could not be repaired. It's kind of funny now, but Danny was pretty pissed off at the time.

After the charges were read at the initial appearance, all the defendants were ordered to be held in custody until a date for a detention hearing was set. A detention hearing, as well as a probable cause hearing, are usually set for the same date, usually within a few business days of the initial appearance. In a detention hearing, a Magistrate will consider arguments concerning a defendant's likelihood to show up at future court proceedings. Should the Magistrate feel that a defendant might flee, or if she feels the defendant is a danger to the community, she can order that person be held in custody without a bond. A probable cause hearing is like a mini-trial where the evidence against a defendant is presented and his attorney is allowed to cross-examine any witnesses testifying to that evidence. If the Magistrate finds probable cause for the charges, the case can proceed. Magistrate Valdez set the same date for both hearings.

In a lot of wiretap cases, defense attorneys will waive their client's right to a probable cause hearing primarily because the determination that probable cause exists is usually a foregone conclusion; after all, the magistrate has already found probable cause exists since she issued the arrest warrants after reading the affidavit detailing the evidence. Sometimes a defense attorney will request a hearing to get an agent on record with sworn testimony. Should that testimony differ in the future from testimony in a trial, the attorney can use that conflicting testimony to discredit a witness.

In this case, every attorney waived his client's rights except Pelon's and Manolo's. Magistrate Valdez would later find probable cause existed to continue with the court proceedings against both Pelon and Manolo.

We spent the next few weeks writing our arrest reports and processing any evidence that had been recovered during searches. We patiently waited to hear from the AUSAs if any defendant wanted to come in and cooperate. Even though there was not much anyone could tell us about the organization that we didn't already know, there was still information that some of them could provide to fill in the gaps of what we did not know. Some of the information we would eventually gather would lead to additional arrests.

Chapter 18

Cheque, Ruben and Ruben's wife had arrived in Chicago sometime around the beginning of 2009. Jorge had been in Michoacan when he was offered a job in Chicago. His role had been to provide the appearance of a family living at the Cambria Court cocaine stash house, while Cheque made deliveries to local customers. When Jorge and his wife and child first arrived in Joliet, Cheque had already been living at the Cambria house for some time. Jorge had never met Cheque prior to arriving at the Joliet residence.

Jorge was to be paid $300 a week, along with the promise of a $35,000 lump sum payment at the conclusion of a year-long tour of duty. He was scheduled to return to Mexico in December of 2009.

Choche's duties overseeing the distribution of cocaine had been terminated sometime after our seizures at the Hickory Hills and Justice stash houses in September of 2008. When he was put in charge of the drug distribution group in Chicago in late 2007 or early 2008, he was given a salary of $5,000 a month. He had also been promised a lump sum payment of $100,000 upon the completion of his tour of duty.

After the seizure of 71 kilograms of cocaine on November 12, 2008, Panda had fled Chicago and went to live with Squert in Wisconsin over the Christmas holiday. We did not know at the time that Panda was using the phone that we had been trying to locate and the informant had been calling to place his order for cocaine. Panda had been suspicious of the informant and he had not wanted the delivery of 25 kilograms to occur.

Felix had ordered the delivery be made. After we arrested the courier and searched the house in Bolingbrook, La Familia bosses, in particular Enrique Plancarte, made arrangements for Panda to flee Chicago and stay with Squert. Squert and Plancarte were both from the same town in Michoacan and Plancarte was the backer who vouched for Squert to receive cocaine in Chicago.

Panda would return to Chicago in late December of 2008 and eventually set up the stash houses on Fairfield and Cambria, as well as his residence on Brookfield. The fact that he had lived with Squert explained why Squert would go to Panda's house during cocaine and money deliveries. Whenever Squert would come to Chicago to deliver money or receive cocaine, he would go to Panda's house while his associate handled the physical exchange of cocaine or money with Ruben or Cheque at another location not far away. Squert was the only cocaine customer who personally knew Panda.

It was at this time that we learned the man we had in custody who we thought was Ponciano was named Celso. The name "Ponciano" had been used by Felix and Panda to refer interchangeably to either Celso or Compadre.

We also filed charges against Ismael's brother-in-law, Beto. Beto had been the person who would let Ismael know if drug money needed to be picked up in Chicago. He would be arrested in October of 2009.

The customer Carlos had obtained his approval to receive cocaine from the man nicknamed "Pelavacas." Pelavacas had spent some time in Chicago but he was now living in Michoacan and had an association with La Familia's leaders Nazario Moreno-Gonzalez and Enrique Plancarte. Carlos would place his orders for cocaine with Pelavacas, who would in turn place that order with La Familia's leaders. The order would be passed onto the drug distribution group in Chicago and the delivery would be made to Carlos. We indicted Pelavacas and in December of 2009 the Mexican police arrested him in Michoacan. Pelavacas would be extradited to Chicago in November of 2012.

In February of 2010, we indicted the real estate agent, Maria, who had been actively involved in obtaining stash houses in Chicago for La Familia crew members. Maria had gone to live in Michoacan in the summer of 2008. We made arrangements with her attorney for her to turn herself in when she returned to Chicago. She returned to the U.S. in August 2010, and on August 5 she made her initial appearance in U.S. District Court in Chicago.

During the wires on Panda's phones, we had intercepted a man named "Guero," who was an associate of Pelon. Guero, while he was in Michoacan, had made the arrangements for Pelon to take delivery of five kilograms of cocaine on May 18, 2009. Guero had come to Chicago near the end of May and had made money deliveries with Pelon to Ruben and Choco but we had not gotten a good look at him during our surveillances. In any event, we learned his identity and discovered that he frequently crossed into the U.S. through a Border Patrol checkpoint near San Diego, California. We felt confident that he would be crossing the border again sometime in the future. On April 23, 2010, we obtained an arrest warrant for him and the warrant was entered into the FBI's national database. The next time he tried to cross the border, the Border Patrol would run his name and discover the outstanding warrant. Sure enough, in September of 2010, Guero tried to cross into the U.S. at the same checkpoint. He was arrested after his name was run through the computer. He would later be extradited to Chicago.

While we were conducting interviews and obtaining additional indictments, we had also initiated a new round of wire intercepts. During our preparations for the customer round-up in August of 2009, we had decided not to charge a customer nicknamed "Monster." Because we did not have as strong a case against Monster as we did against the other customers, we did not charge him, but we also decided that tapping his cellular phones might lead us to new drug suppliers in Chicago. In March of 2010, we obtained court-authorization to tap his phone.

The phone calls we intercepted revealed that he and an associate named "Velasco" were still involved in trafficking cocaine in Chicago. We had hoped the calls would lead to the identification of any new drug or money crews that may have been sent to Chicago to replace Panda. When it didn't appear that this was going to be the case, we decided to seize what we could from Monster's customers and wrap up the investigation.

In April of 2010, we intercepted calls that he was going to deliver three kilograms of heroin and eight kilograms of cocaine to one of his Chicago-based customers. We watched the delivery occur at a park on the north side of Chicago. After the delivery occurred, we followed the customer to the west-bound lanes of Interstate 290. At our request, a Chicago Police tactical unit conducted the stop of the car and they recovered the kilograms of heroin and cocaine from the one male occupant, who was taken into custody.

State charges were filed against that customer while we prepared a criminal complaint charging him, Monster, Velasco, another customer nicknamed "Bone" who was from Chicago Heights, and two others with drug trafficking offenses. In May of 2010, all six individuals would be in federal custody. All six would later plead guilty.

The wiretap of Monster's phone had been somewhat disappointing in that we had not identified any large-scale trafficking organization and we had seized only three kilograms of heroin and eight kilograms of cocaine. However, we had intercepted a tractor-trailer driver, whose nickname was "Mascarita," who appeared to be involved in driving drug loads to Chicago. After the arrest of Monster and his associates, we obtained Mascarita's cell phone records and discovered that he was not only still using the same number we had previously intercepted, it also appeared that he was still travelling to Chicago. At the end of July 2010, we obtained court-authorization to physically track his cellular phone.

On Wednesday, July 28, the cellular location information revealed that Mascarita's phone was in the Los Angeles, California, area. The phone continued to ping there for the next two days.

On Friday afternoon, July 30, the phone began pinging in southern Nevada. Stull continued to check the cell phone's location throughout the day into Saturday. The phone, and Mascarita, continued moving east toward Chicago.

On Sunday morning, August 1, it became apparent that Mascarita would arrive in the Chicago area later in the day. Around the time that Mascarita crossed the Mississippi River into Illinois, he began calling a Chicago phone number, which was a good indication that he was planning to meet someone once he arrived in the Chicago area.

During the wire of Monster's phone, we had watched him meet with Mascarita at a truck stop on Interstate 80 in Morris, Illinois. So, in the late afternoon, several of us drove out to that truck stop with the expectation that Mascarita would likely stop there again. And he did.

At around 7:00 P.M., we watched Mascarita exit Interstate 80 and park his tractor-trailer in the same lot where we had previously seen him meet with Monster. We could not know if Mascarita was delivering cocaine or receiving drug money to transport but we felt confident that he would soon be doing one or the other.

At about 9:00 P.M., a small SUV driven by a lone Hispanic male drove into the lot and stopped just short of Mascarita's tractor-trailer. After a short hesitation, the SUV drove closer and Mascarita got out of the cab of his truck. The lone male exited his SUV at about the same time. As Mascarita was handing the lone male a box and a duffel bag, we drove into the lot. Mascarita saw us coming and began scurrying back to his truck, while the lone male began to slowly walk away from us. We stopped both men and attempted to talk to them but neither man spoke English and we had no Spanish speakers with us at the time. We took a closer look at the SUV and saw a box and a duffel bag sitting on the front passenger seat of the vehicle. The zipper on the duffel bag was not completely closed and we could see the unmistakable shape and size of kilograms of cocaine inside the bag. The box underneath the bag also contained kilograms of cocaine. We would seize a total of 45 kilograms of cocaine.

We searched the tractor-trailer but there was no additional cocaine on board. We would later learn that Mascarita was transporting a legitimate load of cargo and he had concealed the 45 kilograms within some of the boxes that were located halfway into the trailer. Had he been stopped by any state trooper along the way from California to Chicago, he would have had the proper paperwork to give the appearance that he was a legitimate truck driver hauling a legitimate cargo, which he was.

The driver of the SUV, who had been sent to take delivery of the 45 kilograms from Mascarita, would later plead guilty.

Even though we had caught him red-handed and later discovered that his fingerprints were on one of the kilograms, Mascarita decided to take his chances in front of a jury. He was convicted in U.S. District Court on June 13, 2012, and later sentenced to 188 months in prison.

As we conducted interviews, made more arrests, and conducted additional wiretaps throughout 2010, the violence continued in Michoacan. On June 14, 2010, La Familia gunmen ambushed a convoy of Mexican federal police on a highway near the city of Ziticuaro. The ambush resulted in the killing of ten officers and the wounding of several others.

Five of our defendants would plead guilty throughout 2010. The customer Carlos was the first to plead guilty to drug conspiracy charges. He pled guilty in April of 2010 and he was sentenced to 100 months in prison on July 28, 2015.

The customer Saul had already been in federal custody when we conducted our round-ups in August of 2009. He pled guilty in May of 2010 and was sentenced on the same day to 120 months in prison.

The drug distribution group supervisor Choche also pled guilty in May and he would be sentenced to 155 months in prison on September 23, 2014.

The first customer we had identified in this case, Manolo pled guilty in August of 2010. He would be sentenced to 92 months in prison on March 30, 2011. His sentence would be reduced to 73 months in January of 2015.

The customer Pelon, who worked with Guero, was the last to plead guilty in 2010. He pled on October 15, 2010. He would be sentenced in December of 2011 to 46 months in prison.

On December 9, 2010, in Michoacan, Mexican government forces engaged in a two-day gun battle with La Familia members near the city of Apatzingan. After the battle, the government announced that Nazario "el Chayo" Moreno had been killed even though his body had not been recovered. Mendez-Vargas ("el Chango") reportedly fought for control of La Familia, resulting in a power struggle with Servando Gomez and Enrique Plancarte. Gomez formed his own group which called itself the "Knights Templar," named after the group of knights who protected pilgrims during trips to the Holy Land during the Crusades. Rumors persisted that Moreno had not been killed and that he was in charge, along with Gomez and Plancarte, of the new group. He was, in fact, still alive.

At the end of 2010, we had completed the bulk of our wiretaps. With the investigation nearly complete, we would spend most of our time conducting interviews, making more arrests, and preparing for the trials of those who chose not to plead guilty.

Chapter 19

Jorge, the member of the drug distribution group under Panda, was the first to plead guilty in 2011. He pled on January 4. He would be sentenced to 64 months in prison on October 25, 2013.

The customer "El Gato," and associate of Jesse, pled guilty in February. He would be sentenced to 60 months in prison on May 13.

The money courier Ismael pled guilty on February 16. He would be sentenced to 67 months in June of 2013. His sentence was later reduced to 54 months in May of 2015.

Ismael's assistant, Oscar, pled guilty in March. He would be sentenced in June to 63 months in prison. His sentence would be reduced to 51 months in March of 2015.

On March 8, Panda pled guilty. He would be sentenced in August to 480 months in prison. That sentence would be reduced in April of 2014 to 350 months. We would learn a little about his circumstances during his resentencing hearing in 2014. During the hearing, his attorney said that Panda was from Apatzingan, Michoacan. The attorney said that La Familia was having difficulties recruiting new members in 2007. Panda was offered a job with La Familia and he was given the choice of working for them in the United States or in Mexico. Panda chose to work in the U.S. The attorney also stated that La Familia members made threats against Panda's family to get him to work, which may or may not be true. As AUSA Bhachu would point out, Panda had not made that coercion claim at his first sentencing hearing. Panda claimed he had been paid $2,000 a month during his tenure overseeing the drug and money crews in Chicago. When he was asked by the judge if he wanted to say anything before he was resentenced, Panda made the following statement in Spanish: "That I want you to give me the opportunity to demonstrate that I am not the person who they say I am. My only desire is to be able to return soon to be with my family and never to set foot again in this place in the United States for any reason. And I ask for forgiveness for all of this that has happened. Thank you." Panda was 42 years old at the time of his sentencing.

On March 11, the real estate agent Maria pled guilty. She would be sentenced to 18 months in prison on August 27, 2013.

On March 14, the drug distribution courier Cheque pled guilty. He would be sentenced in September to 264 months in prison.

The customer Celso, who we had originally believed was named Ponciano, pled guilty on March 25. He would be sentenced in August to 57 months in prison.

The customer Edwin, who was a customer of Carlos, pled guilty on April 12. He would be sentenced in October to 262 months in prison. The lengthiness of his sentence was based on his previous criminal record. His sentence would later be reduced to 210 months.

We discovered that the wife of money crew member Ruben had moved into a residence near Los Angeles, California. We had to let Ruben go in June of 2009 for strategic legal reasons. Knowing that Ruben and his wife had an infant child, we figured the odds were good that Ruben had returned from Mexico and was probably living with her. In fact, he had already been stopped once by the Border Patrol trying to re-enter the U.S. We figured he would succeed in crossing the border and return to his wife and child, so we filed charges against him at the end of 2009. The U.S. Marshals Service arrested him in May of 2011 at the wife's residence where we suspected he would be. He was later extradited to Chicago.

On June 14, the customer Anai pled guilty. She would be sentenced to 70 months in prison on November 16.

Meanwhile in Mexico, Mexican federal police arrested La Familia's former number-two man, Jesus "el Chango" Mendez-Vargas, in the state of Aguascalientes on June 21, 2011. Mendez remains in custody, pending his potential extradition to New York City to face charges. After his arrest, the Mexican Attorney General announced on August 7, 2011, that the La Familia cartel was disbanded. The leaders of the Knights Templar, Gomez and Plancarte, were still at large. The rumors persisted that Moreno had not been killed by Mexican forces and that he was actually in control of the Knights Templar.

In September, the customer Guero, the associate of Pelon, chose not to plead guilty and went to trial. A jury in federal court found him guilty on September 29, 2011. He was sentenced on February 4, 2013, to 168 months in prison.

In November, the customer Jesse would be the last to plead guilty in 2011. He would be sentenced on June 8, 2012, to 120 months in prison.

The customer Squert had initially intended to go to trial. After several trial dates were postponed for varying reasons, Squert changed his mind and pled guilty on May 24, 2012. He would be sentenced in June of 2013 to 81 months in prison.

Beto, the brother-in-law of the money courier Ismael, went to trial in November of 2012. He was found guilty by a federal jury on November 14. He would be sentenced in May of 2013 to 360 months in prison. He appealed his conviction and the U.S. Court of Appeals reversed the conviction and remanded the case back to the District Court in June of 2015. Beto was tried again in August of 2016 and was found guilty again in September. He would be sentenced in April of 2018 to 240 months in prison.

On March 4, 2013, money crew member Ruben pled guilty. He would be sentenced in May to 54 months in prison. Ruben was the first and last defendant to plead guilty in 2013.

In March of 2014, the rumors that Moreno had not been killed in December of 2010 were proved to be true. On March 9, Mexican government forces attempted to arrest Moreno in the city of Tumbiscatio in Michoacan. Moreno opened fire and in the ensuing gun fight, he was killed. This time the government recovered his body and DNA and fingerprint examinations confirmed his identity.

On March 19, Javier, the associate of Celso and Compadre, was arrested. He had been a fugitive ever since our charges were filed in August of 2009. He pled guilty the following year and was sentenced to 57 months in prison on August 5, 2015.

On March 31, 2014, Enrique Plancarte, a Knights Templar leader and the backer for the customer Squert, was killed in a gun battle with Mexican government forces in the state of Queretaro. Servando Gomez, the last remaining leader of the Knights Templar group, was next on the government's target list.

After being extradited to Chicago from Mexico, Pelavacas, who was the backer for the customer Carlos, pled guilty on July 16, 2014. He was sentenced to 126 months in prison on December 2, 2014.

In February of 2015, Mexican federal police identified a location in Michoacan's capital city of Morelia where they believed Gomez was hiding. The location was pinpointed after police observed Gomez' girlfriend deliver a chocolate cake to his hideout on his birthday, which was February 6. On February 27, Gomez was arrested in an operation where no shots were fired. He remains in custody in Mexico. Shortly after his arrest, Mexican government authorities announced that the Knights Templar group had been mostly disbanded.

In May of 2014, Carlos Rosales, one of the original founders of the cartel group "La Empresa" (The Company) - the group that preceded La Familia – was released from a Mexican prison. On December 28, 2015, he and three others were found shot to death near a highway in Michoacan.

Throughout the course of our investigation of the La Familia cartel in Chicago, we had seized over 8.9 million dollars, 373 kilograms of cocaine, and three kilograms of heroin. We had arrested 31 individuals, all of whom have pled guilty or been found guilty at trial. There are three defendants whose whereabouts remain unknown.

The whereabouts of Felix, the man who was in charge of the Chicago drug and money crews from 2007 through 2009, remains unknown.

Acknowledgements and Sources

Much of the information that I used to write this book, such as the intercepted phone calls and law enforcement seizures, came from open court records available in U.S District Court in the Northern District of Illinois. For the section that told the story of the investigation into the Engineer's organization, I used documents from the following court docket cases: 03 CR 0670, 03 CR 1136, 04 CR 0200, 04 CR 0219, 04 CR 0286, 04 CR 0387, and 04 CR 0751. I also used documents from U.S. District Court in the District of Colorado, under court docket number 03 CR 0615.

I also used, to a lesser extent, open source information such as contemporary news accounts of the people or events described in the book. Furthermore, I relied upon my own recollections of the events that I participated in. Any errors of fact are solely my responsibility.

For the section detailing the investigation into the La Familia Michoacana drug cartel, I relied upon open court records in U.S. District Court, Northern District of Illinois, under the following docket numbers: 09 CR 0546, 09 CR 0558, 09 CR 0716, 09 CR 0964, 09 CR 0965, 09 CR 0966, 09 CR 0967, 09 CR 0968, 09 CR 0969. 09 CR 0997, 09 CR 1043, 09 CR 1044, 10 CR 0131, 10 CR 0333, and 10 CR 0652. I also used open source, contemporaneous news accounts of the people and events described in the book, as well as my own recollections of the events that I participated in. Again, any errors of fact are my responsibility.

I want to acknowledge the Assistant U.S. Attorneys, Special Agents and Task Force Officers who made both cases possible. They were all, without exception, a pleasure to work with in every circumstance. In no particular order, I'd like to recognize AUSAs Morris Pasqual, Chris Niewoehner, Daniel Collins, Lisa Noller, Amar Bhachu, Michael Donovan, Stephen Baker, Megan Church and Erika Csicsila.

I also want to acknowledge all the agents and police officers who participated in the surveillances, seizures and arrests that were conducted in both cases. It was an awesome experience to work with everybody. Since I can't name everyone, I'd like to specifically acknowledge, in no particular order, Tim McCormick, Scott Weinstein, Rich Young, James Jones, Neeshan Tulshi, Tim McQuillen, Ron Brenza, Mike Benaitis, the late Pete Michaels, Jerry Wodka, Jeff Werniak, Paul Roach, Keith Bishop, William "Curt" Fallin, Kirk Seeley, Luke McConnell, Nick Stull, Mike Mokhoff, Keith Landa, Jim Chupik, Will Taylor, Ty Collins, Colin Dickey, Danny Gutierrez, Rudy Avalos, Rich Sperando and Darlinda Rodriguez. If I've forgotten anyone, I sincerely apologize.

I also want to thank former AUSAs Kevin Powers and Larry Beaumont for their guidance and advice.

I'd also like to thank the people at "The Bookmakers," who made this book dream a reality. It was a pleasure to work with Joel Friedlander, Abigail Dunard, Tracy Atkins and my editor, Treana Atkins.

And, finally, I'd like to thank my wife, Adrianna, who always supported my efforts and was extremely patient (most of the time) with the hundreds of pages of documents and records that I left scattered throughout the house.

About the Author

The author spent 26 years with the U.S. Drug Enforcement Administration, retiring as a Supervisory Special Agent in 2014.

www.ingramcontent.com/pod-product-compliance
Lightning Source LLC
Chambersburg PA
CBHW020414080526
44584CB00014B/1325